Preparing Students
for
Success and Leadership
in
College and Careers

by

Susanna Palomares
Dianne Schilling
David Cowan

Cover design: Dave Cowan

ISBN-10: 1-56499-093-1

ISBN-13: 978-1-56499-093-8

INNERCHOICE Publishing
15079 Oak Chase Court
Wellington, FL 33414

Contents

INTRODUCTION

All over the nation, innovative changes have been initiated to improve the quality of education and to prepare students for success in a rapidly evolving world. *Preparing Students for Success and Leadership in College and Careers* supports these initiatives by providing the social-emotional and skill development components necessary for a fulfilling, productive experience through school, into work life, and beyond.

What does it take for young people to be college and career ready so that they find success and are able to take the lead when necessary? Today's students will need to succeed and lead in a highly competitive global economy, a knowledge-based society, and hyper-connected digital age. Of course, students must have specific knowledge and skill in many areas. Academic and STEAM programs provide important avenues for students to acquire that knowledge. However, beyond the academic and technical, students must also develop employability skills like effective communications and conversational abilities, problem solving, critical thinking, goal setting and attainment, self-determination and personal mastery, teamwork and collaboration, etc. These are the skills that businesses are looking for in their employees. These skills also provide a firm foundation of awareness, behaviors, and abilities that enable young people to survive and thrive in school, work, and life endeavors. The activities, Sharing Circles, and Experience Sheets in *Preparing Students for Success and Leadership in College and Careers* are designed to develop all these important life skills in an active and engaging learning environment.

Interest and enthusiasm fire learning.

A variety of activities and strategies have been incorporated into *Preparing Students for Success and Leadership in College and Careers*. You will find discussions, simulations, experiments, games, drama, creative writing, research, and much more. Perhaps the most significant strategy is the Sharing Circle, a unique small-group discussion process in which participants share their experiences, thoughts, and feelings in a safe, structured environment. Besides developing self-awareness, social and communication skills, the Sharing Circle encourages participants to appreciate likenesses and celebrate diversity, and it is a model of inclusion and interdependence. Sharing Circles provide a perfect environment for students to relate authentically and to feel socially connected.

As an instructional tool, the purpose of the Sharing Circle is to promote growth and development in students of all ages and abilities. Targeted growth areas include communication, self-awareness, personal mastery, and interpersonal skills. As students follow the rules and relate to each other verbally during the Sharing Circle, they are practicing oral communication and learning to listen. Through insights developed in the course of pondering and discussing the various topics, students are offered the opportunity to grow in awareness and to feel more masterful—more in control of their feelings, thoughts, and behaviors. Through the positive experience of give and take, they learn more about effective modes of social interaction. The Sharing Circle provides practice in the use of basic communication skills while relevant life issues are being discussed and valuable concepts learned.

Every activity and Sharing Circle concludes with a set of discussion questions formulated to facilitate the cognitive process. These discussion questions give young people a chance to share observations and insights; they provide an opportunity to analyze, make comparisons, and express personal feelings. Discussion questions give the learner a chance to consider various applications of newly acquired knowledge, skills, and tools. They invite the learner to develop new expectations and goals for the future. Discussion questions connect abstract learnings to real-life situations. Although several discussion questions are provided with each activity and Sharing Circle, we also encourage you to ask additional questions based on your experiences, those of the students, and the flow of the discussion itself.

Through discussion and interaction, learners are given the opportunity to connect the information to their own lives to see how and where it fits and how to make appropriate applications. The format of learning encouraged by the design of the experiences in this curriculum guide is facilitated by creating situations in which information is presented, modelled, practiced, and then discussed with regard to its relevance to the learners.

How to Set Up Sharing Circles

Group Size and Composition

Sharing Circles are a time for focusing on students' contributions in an unhurried fashion. For this reason, each Sharing Circle group needs to be kept relatively small—eight to twelve usually works best. In high school students are capable of extensive verbalization. You will want to encourage this, and not stifle them because of time constraints.

Each group should be as heterogeneous as possible with respect to sex, ability, and racial/ethnic background. Sometimes there will be a group in which all the students are particularly reticent to speak. At these times, bring in an expressive student or two who will get things going. Sometimes it is necessary for practical reasons to change the membership of a group. Once established, however, it is advisable to keep a group as stable as possible.

Length and Location of Sharing Circles

Depending on the number and the verbal expressiveness of the students in a Sharing Circle, some circle sessions can last 20 to 30 minutes. At first, students tend to be reluctant to express themselves fully because they do not yet know that the circle is a safe place. Consequently your first sessions may not last more than 10 to 15 minutes. Generally speaking, students become comfortable and motivated to speak with continued experience.

Sharing Circles may be conducted at any time during the class period. Starting circle sessions at the beginning of the period allows additional time in case students become deeply involved in the topic. If you start circles late in the period, make sure the students are aware of their responsibility to be concise.

Sharing Circles may be carried out wherever there is room for students to sit in a circle and experience few or no distractions. Some leaders prefer to have students sit in chairs, others on the floor. Some leaders conduct sessions outdoors, with students seated in a secluded, grassy area.

How to Get Started

Teachers and counselors have used numerous methods to involve students in the circle process. What works well for one leader or class does not always work for another. Here are two basic strategies leaders have successfully used to set up Sharing Circle groups. Whichever you use, we recommend that you post a chart listing the Sharing Circle rules and procedures to which every participant may refer.

1. Start one group at a time, and cycle through all groups. If possible, provide an opportunity for every student to experience a Sharing Circle in a setting where there are no disturbances. This may mean arranging for another staff member or aide to take charge of the students not participating in the circle. Non-participants may work on course work or silent reading, or, if you have a cooperative media specialist, they may be sent to the media center to work independently or in small groups on a class assignment. Repeat this procedure until all of the students have been involved in at least one Sharing Circle.

Next, initiate a class discussion about the circle sessions. Explain that from now on you will be meeting with each Sharing Circle group in the classroom, with the remainder of the class present. Ask the students to help you plan established procedures for the remainder of the class to follow.

Meet with each Sharing Circle group on a different day, systematically cycling through the groups. You may wish to start student leadership training after you've completed a number of circles. In each group, allow a student the opportunity to lead the session as you sit beside him or her, acting as leader-trainer. In time, student-led groups may meet independently at staggered times during the period, or they may meet simultaneously in different parts of the room while you circulate. Eventually you should be able to be a participant in the student-led groups. For more information on student leadership, refer to the next chapter, "Training Student Leaders."

2. Combine inner and outer circles. Meet with one Sharing Circle group while another group listens and observes as an outer circle. Then have the two groups change places, with the students on the outside becoming the inner circle, and responding verbally to the topic. If you run out of time, use two class periods for this. Later, a third group may be added to this alternating cycle. The end product of this arrangement is two or more groups (comprising everyone in the class) meeting together simultaneously. While one group is involved in discussion, the other groups listen and observe as members of an outer circle. *Invite the members of the outer circle to participate in the discussion phase of the circle.*

What To Do With the Rest of the Class

If you are working with a classroom or large group of students, a number of arrangements can be made for students who are not participating in Sharing Circles. Here are some ideas:

- Have students work quietly on subject-area assignments in pairs or small, task-oriented groups.
- Utilize student aides or leaders. If the seat-work activity is in a content area, appoint students who show ability in that area as "consultants," and have them assist other students.
- Give the students plenty to do. List academic activities on the board. Make

materials for quiet individual activities available so that students cannot run out of things to do and be tempted to consult you or disturb others.

- Make the activity of students outside the Sharing Circle enjoyable. When you can involve the rest of the class in something meaningful to them, students will probably be less likely to interrupt the circle.
- Have the students work on an ongoing project. When they have a task in progress, students can simply resume where they left off, with little or no introduction from you. In these cases, appointing a "person in charge," "group leader," or "consultant" is wise.
- Allow individual journal-writing. While a Sharing Circle is in progress, have the other students make entries in a private (or share-with-teacher/counselor-only) journal. The topic for journal writing could be the same topic that is being discussed in the Sharing Circle. Do not correct the journals, but if you read them, be sure to respond to the entries with your own written thoughts, where appropriate.

How to Lead a Sharing Circle

This section is a thorough guide for conducting Sharing Circles. It covers major points to keep in mind and answers questions which will arise as you begin using the program. Please remember that these guidelines are presented to assist you, not to restrict you. Follow them, and trust your own leadership style at the same time.

The Sharing Circle is a structured communication process that provides students a safe place for learning about life and developing important aspects of social-emotional learning.

First, we'll provide a brief overview of the process of leading a Sharing Circle and then we'll cover each step in more detail.

A Sharing Circle begins when a group of students and the adult leader sit down together in a circle so that each person is able to see the others easily. The leader of the Sharing Circle briefly greets and welcomes each individual, conveying a feeling of enthusiasm blended with seriousness.

When everyone appears comfortable, the leader takes a few moments to review the Sharing Circle Rules. These rules inform the students of the positive behaviors required of them and guarantees the emotional safety and security, and equality of each member.

After the students understand and agree to follow the rules, the leader announces the topic for the session. A brief elaboration of the topic follows in which the leader provides examples and possibly mentions the topics relationship to prior topics or to other things the students are involved in. Then the leader re-states the topic and allows a little silence during which circle members may review and ponder their own related memories and mentally prepare their verbal response to the topic. (The topics and elaborations are provided in this curriculum.)

Next, the leader invites the circle participants to voluntarily share their responses to the topic, one at a time. No one is forced to share, but everyone is given an opportunity to share while all the other circle members listen attentively. The circle participants tell the group about themselves, their personal experiences, thoughts, feelings, hopes and dreams as they relate to the topic. Most of the circle time is devoted to this sharing phase because of its central importance.

During this time, the leader assumes a dual role—that of leader and participant. The leader makes sure that everyone who wishes to speak is given the opportunity while simultaneously enforcing the rules as necessary. The leader also takes a turn to speak if he or she wishes.

After everyone who wants to share has done so, the leader introduces the next phase of the Sharing Circle by asking several discussion questions. This phase represents a transition to the intellectual mode and allows participants to reflect on and express learnings gained from the sharing phase and encourages participants to combine cognitive abilities and emotional experiencing. It's in this phase that participants are able to crystallize learnings and to understand the relevance of the discussion to their daily lives. (Discussion questions for each topic are provided in this curriculum.)

When the students have finished discussing their responses to the questions and the session has reached a natural closure, the leader ends the session. The leader thanks the students for being part of the Sharing Circle and states that it is over.

What follows is a more detailed look at the process of leading a Sharing Circle.

Steps for Leading a Sharing Circle

1. **Welcome Sharing Circle members**
2. **Review the Sharing Circle rules ***
3. **Introduce the topic**
4. **Sharing by circle members**
5. **Ask discussion questions**
6. **Close the circle**

   ***optional after the first few sessions**

1. Welcome Sharing Circle members

As you sit down with the students in a Sharing Circle group, remember that you are not teaching a lesson. You are facilitating a group of people. Establish a positive atmosphere. In a relaxed manner, address each student by name, using eye contact and conveying warmth. An attitude of seriousness blended with enthusiasm will let the students know that this Sharing Circle group is an important learning experience—an activity that can be interesting and meaningful.

2. Review the Sharing Circle rules

At the beginning of the first Sharing Circle, and at appropriate intervals thereafter, go over the rules for the circle. They are:

Sharing Circle Rules

- **Everyone gets a turn to share, including the leader.**
- **You can skip your turn if you wish.**
- **Listen to the person who is sharing.**
- **There are no interruptions, probing, put-downs, or gossip.**
- **Share the time equally.**

From this point on, demonstrate to the students that you expect them to remember and abide by the ground rules. Convey that you think well of them and know they are fully capable of responsible behavior. Let them know that by coming to the Sharing Circle they are making a commitment to listen and show acceptance and respect for the other students and you. It is helpful to write the rules on chart paper and keep them on display for the benefit of each Sharing Circle session.

3. Introduce the topic

State the topic, and then in your own words, elaborate and provide examples as each lesson in this book suggests. The introduction or elaboration of the topic is designed to get students focused and thinking about how they will respond to the topic. By providing more than just the mere statement of the topic, the elaboration gives students a few moments to expand their thinking and to make a personal connection to the topic at hand. Add clarifying statements of your own that will help the students understand the topic. Answer questions about the topic, and emphasize that there are no "right" responses. Finally, restate the topic, opening the session to responses (theirs and yours). Sometimes taking your turn first helps the students understand the aim of the topic. The introductions, as written in this book, are provided to give you some general ideas for opening the Sharing Circle. It's important that you adjust and modify the introduction and elaboration to suit the ages, abilities, levels, cultural/ethnic backgrounds and interests of your students.

4. Sharing by circle members

The most important point to remember is this: The purpose of these Sharing Circles is to give students an opportunity to express themselves and be accepted for the experiences, thoughts, and feelings they share. Avoid taking the action away from the students. They are the stars!

5. Ask discussion questions

Responding to discussion questions is the cognitive portion of the process. During this phase, the leader asks thought-provoking questions to stimulate free discussion and higher-level thinking. Each Sharing Circle lesson in this book concludes with several discussion questions. At times, you may want to formulate questions that are more appropriate to the level of understanding in your students—or to what was actually shared in the circle. If you wish to make connections between the topic and your content area, ask questions that will accomplish that objective and allow the answering of the discussion questions to extend longer.

6. Close the circle

The ideal time to end a Sharing Circle is when the discussion question phase reaches natural closure. Sincerely thank everyone for being part of the circle. Don't thank specific students for speaking, as doing so might convey the impression that speaking is more appreciated than mere listening. Then close the group by saying, "This Sharing Circle is over," or "OK, that ends our circle."

More about Sharing Circle Steps and Rules

The next few paragraphs offer further clarification concerning leadership of Sharing Circles.

Who gets to talk? Everyone. The importance of acceptance cannot be overly stressed. In one way or another practically every ground rule says one thing: accept one another. When you model acceptance of students, they will learn how to be accepting. Each individual in the group is important and deserves a turn to speak if he or she wishes to take it. Equal opportunity to become involved should be given to everyone in the Sharing Circle.

Members should be reinforced equally for their contributions. There are many reasons why a leader may become more enthused over what one student shares than another. The response may be more on target, reflect more depth, be more entertaining, be philosophically more in keeping with one's own point of view, and so on. However, students need to be given equal recognition for their contributions, even if the contribution is to listen silently throughout the session.

In most of the Sharing Circles, plan to take a turn and address the topic, too. Students usually appreciate it very much and learn a great deal when their teachers, counselors, and other adults are willing to tell about their own experiences, thoughts, and feelings. In this way you let your students know that you acknowledge your own humanness.

Does everyone have to take a turn? No. Students may choose to skip their turns. If the circle becomes a pressure situation in which the members are coerced in any way to speak, it will become an unsafe place where participants are not comfortable. Meaningful discussion is unlikely in such an atmosphere. By allowing students to make this choice, you are showing them that you accept their right to remain silent if that is what they choose to do.

As you begin the circle, it's important to remember that it's not a problem if one or more students decline to speak. If you are imperturbable and accepting when this happens, you let them know you are offering them an opportunity to experience something you think is valuable, or at least worth a try, and not attempting to force-feed them. You as a leader should not feel compelled to share a personal experience in every session, either. However, if you decline to speak in most of the sessions, this may have an inhibiting effect on the students' willingness to share.

A word should also be said about how this ground rule has sometimes been carried to extremes. Sometimes leaders have bent over backwards to let students know they don't have to take a turn. This seeming lack of enthusiasm on the part of the leader has caused reticence in the students. In order to avoid this outcome, don't project any personal insecurity as you lead the session. Be confident in your proven ability to work with students. Expect something to happen and it will.

Some leaders ask the participants to raise their hands when they wish to speak, while others simply allow free verbal sharing without soliciting the leader's permission first. Choose the procedure that works best for you, but do not call on anyone unless you can see signs of readiness. And do not merely go around the circle.

Some leaders have reported that their first group fell flat—that no one, or just one or two students, had anything to say. But they continued to have groups, and at a certain point everything changed. Thereafter, the students had a great deal to say that these leaders considered worth waiting for. It appears that in these cases the leaders' acceptance of the right to skip turns was a key factor. In time most students will contribute verbally when they have something they want to say, and when they are assured there is no pressure to do so.

Sometimes a silence occurs during a session. Don't feel you have to jump in every time someone stops talking. During silences students have an opportunity to think about what they would like to share or to contemplate an important idea they've heard. A general rule of thumb is to allow silence to the point that you observe group discomfort. At that point move on. Do not switch to another topic. To do so implies you will not be satisfied until the students speak. If you change to another topic, you are telling them you didn't really mean it when you said they didn't have to take a turn if they didn't want to.

If you are bothered about students who attend a number of sessions and still do not share verbally, reevaluate what you consider to be involvement. Participation does not necessarily mean talking. Students who do not speak are listening and learning.

How can I encourage effective listening? The Sharing Circle is a time (and place) for students and leaders to strengthen the habit of listening by doing it over and over again. No one was born knowing how to listen effectively to others. It is a skill like any other that gets better as it is practiced. In the immediacy of the Sharing Circle the members become keenly aware of the necessity to listen, and most students respond by expecting it of one another.

In these Sharing Circles, listening is defined as the respectful focusing of attention on individual speakers. It includes eye contact with the speaker and open body posture. It eschews interruptions of any kind. When you lead a circle, listen and encourage listening in the students by (1) focusing your attention on the person who is speaking, (2) being receptive to what the speaker is saying (not mentally planning your next remark), and (3) recognizing the speaker when she finishes speaking, either verbally ("Thanks, Shirley") or nonverbally (a nod and a smile).

To encourage effective listening in the students, reinforce them by letting them know you have noticed they were listening to each other and you appreciate it.

How can I ensure the students get equal time? When group members share the time equally, they demonstrate their acceptance of the notion that everyone's contribution is of equal importance. It is not uncommon to have at least one dominator in a group. This person is usually totally unaware that by continuing to talk he or she is taking time from others who are less assertive. An important social skill is knowing how you affect others in a group and when dominating a group is inappropriate behavior.

Be very clear with the students about the purpose of this ground rule. Tell them at the outset how much time there is. When it is your turn, always limit your own contribution. If someone goes on and on, do intervene (dominators need to know what they are doing), but do so as gently and respectfully as you can.

What are some examples of put-downs? Put-downs convey the message, "You are not okay as you are." Some put-downs are deliberate, but many are made unknowingly. Both kinds are undesirable in a Sharing Circle because they destroy the atmosphere of acceptance and disrupt the flow of sharing and discussion. Typical put-downs include:

- over questioning.
- statements that have the effect of teaching or preaching
- advice giving
- one-upsmanship
- criticism, disapproval, or objections
- sarcasm
- statements or questions of disbelief

How can I deal with put-downs? There are two major ways for dealing with put-downs: preventing them from occurring and intervening when they do.

Going over the rules with the students at the beginning of each Sharing Circle, particularly in the earliest sessions, is a helpful preventive technique. Another is to reinforce the students when they adhere to the rule. Be sure to use non patronizing, non evaluative language. Unacceptable behavior should be stopped the moment it is recognized by the leader. When you become aware that a put-down is occurring, do whatever you ordinarily do to stop destructive behavior. If one student gives another an unasked-for bit of advice, say for example, "Jane, please give Alicia a chance to tell her story." To a student who interrupts say, "Ed, it's Sally's turn." In most cases the fewer words, the better—students automatically tune out messages delivered as lectures.

Sometimes students disrupt the group by starting a private conversation with the person next to them. Touch the offender on the arm or shoulder while continuing to give eye contact to the student who is speaking. If you can't reach the offender, simply remind him or her of the rule about listening.

If students persist in putting others down or disrupt the circle, ask to see them at another time and hold a brief one-to-one conference, urging them to follow the rules. Suggest that they reconsider their membership in the group. Make it clear that if they don't intend to honor the rules, they are not to come to the group.

How can I keep students from gossiping? Periodically remind students that using names and sharing embarrassing information in a Sharing Circle is not acceptable. Urge the students to relate personally to one another, but not to tell intimate details of their lives.

What should the leader do during the discussion question phase? Conduct this part of the process as an open forum, giving students the opportunity to discuss a variety of ideas and accept those that make sense to them. Don't impose your opinions on the students, or allow the students to impose theirs on one another. Ask open-ended questions, encourage higher-level thinking, contribute your own ideas when appropriate, and act as a facilitator.

In Conclusion: The Two Most Important Things to Remember

No matter what happens in a Sharing Circle session, the following two elements are the most critical:

1. Everyone gets a turn.
2. Everyone who takes a turn gets listened to with respect.

What does it mean to get a turn? Imagine a pie divided into as many pieces as there are people in the group. Telling the students that everyone gets a turn, whether they want to take it or not, is like telling them that each one gets a piece of the pie. Some students may not want their piece right away, but they know it's there to take when they do want it. As the teacher or counselor, you must protect this shared ownership. Getting a turn not only represents a chance to talk, it is an assurance that every member of the group has a "space" that no one else will violate.

When students take their turn, they will be listened to. There will be no attempt by anyone to manipulate what a student is offering. That is, the student will not be probed, interrupted, interpreted, analyzed, put-down, joked-at, advised, preached to, and so on. To "listen to" is to respectfully focus attention on the speaker and to let the speaker know that you have heard what he or she has said.

In the final analysis, the only way that a Sharing Circle can be evaluated is against these two criteria. Thus, if only two students choose to speak, but are listened to—even if they don't say very "deep" or "meaningful" things—the discussion group can be considered a success.

Training Student Leaders

A basic assumption of the Sharing Circle process is that every human being (barring those having considerable subnormal intelligence) has leadership potential. Adolescence is an optimum time to encourage and develop the skills needed for effective leadership Students in countless secondary classrooms skillfully lead their own circle sessions.

You can begin training student leaders after two or three successful circle sessions. Invite the students to consider volunteering to lead a Sharing Circle. Suggest that they watch you closely to see what steps the leader follows. At the end of the session, ask the students to describe what you did. They should be able to delineate the following steps:

The leader:
1. announces the topic and clarifies what it is about.
2. may lead a review of the Sharing Circle rules.
3. gives each person a turn who wants one.
4. asks discussion questions.
5. closes the circle.

Ask the students if anyone would like to volunteer to lead the next session. If no one volunteers, accept this outcome and wait for a session or two before trying again. If several volunteer, choose a student who you think is very likely to succeed. Then tell the group the topic you have in mind for the next session.

Before the next session, give the student leader a copy of the Sharing Circle, and discuss it with him or her. Also provide a copy of the Sharing Circle rules and Steps for Leading the Sharing Circle (see **"How to Lead a Sharing Circle"**). As the session begins, tell the group that you will be the trainer and speak about the process when necessary, but that otherwise, the student is the leader and you are a participant. Before turning the session over to the student leader add one more thing—a new ground rule stating that the students are expected to respect fully the leadership position of the student. **If they disagree with the student leader's procedure or are aware of what he or she should do next when the student leader may have forgotten, they are not to say anything at that time unless they are asked to by the student leader.** When people are learning a new skill, it can be very upsetting to have other people constantly reminding them of what they are supposed to do next. For this reason the student leader should not be heckled in any way. (Time can be taken at the end of the session for the group to give feedback and to thank the student leader for his or her performance).

Now, allow the student leader to proceed, interjecting statements yourself about the procedure only when absolutely necessary. Be sure to take your turn and model respectful listening. As necessary, deal with students who interrupt or distract the group.

Before ending the session, thank the student leader, and conduct a brief feedback session by asking the students, "Who would like to tell (the student leader) what you liked about the way he or she conducted the session?" Let the student leader call on each person who has a comment.

Tell the students the topic you have in mind for the next session, and ask for a volunteer to lead it. Remember that students should not lead the group until you are sure they will be successful. Be careful to appoint leaders of both sexes and all racial/ethnic groups. Continue this process until all who wish to conduct a Sharing Circle are competent enough to lead them independently.

SELF-AWARENESS AND SELF-ESTEEM

Through the development of intrapersonal skills, successful people and potential leaders get to know who they are and what they have to contribute. Self-awareness leads to the development of an accurate self-concept and the ability to effectively manage one's thoughts and actions leads to a positive sense of self-esteem. Learning to understand feelings and their relationship to thoughts is an important component of self-management. Young people need to understand that their feelings are normal, predictable, and susceptible to control. In addition, feelings convey messages about conditions and events going on in the environment, and provide important clues to the way the brain is processing information. Learning to understand feelings is a key to self-control. Another dimension of self-management skills is self-talk. Self-talk is a category of thought that not only shapes self-concept, but predisposes individuals to succeed or fail. Young people need to learn how to control the messages they give themselves about their own abilities and futures.

Activities in this unit concentrate on developing self-managment skills beginning with an awareness of feelings, thoughts, behaviors, values, influences, and accomplishments, and provide young people opportunities to develop constructive habits of self-talk, self-control, and anger management.

All About Me
Experience Sheet and Discussion

Objectives:

The students will:
— identify likes and dislikes and areas of strength and weakness.
— clarify personal values.
— explain how self awareness facilitates goal setting.

Materials:

a copy of the experience sheet "Getting to Know Myself"

Directions:

Pass out the experience sheets and have the students answer the questions. When they have finished, facilitate a class discussion using these and other discussion questions that arise as the discussion progresses.

Discussion Questions:

1. *What have you learned about your strengths and weaknesses from this activity?*

2. *What have you learned about your likes and dislikes?*

3. *What insights did you gain concerning your values?*

4. *How will knowing these kinds of things about yourself help you in school, in college, or in making a career choice?*

5. *How will knowing these things help you be a more effective leader?*

Getting to Know Myself
Experience Sheet

How well do you know yourself? That may seem like a simple question, but everyone has many dimensions. In order to know who you really are you need an accurate sense of self-understanding. You need to be aware of such things as your strengths and limitations, likes and dislikes, wants and needs, beliefs and values. To help get more in touch with who you are in all these dimensions answer the following questions and then spend some time reflecting on your answers.

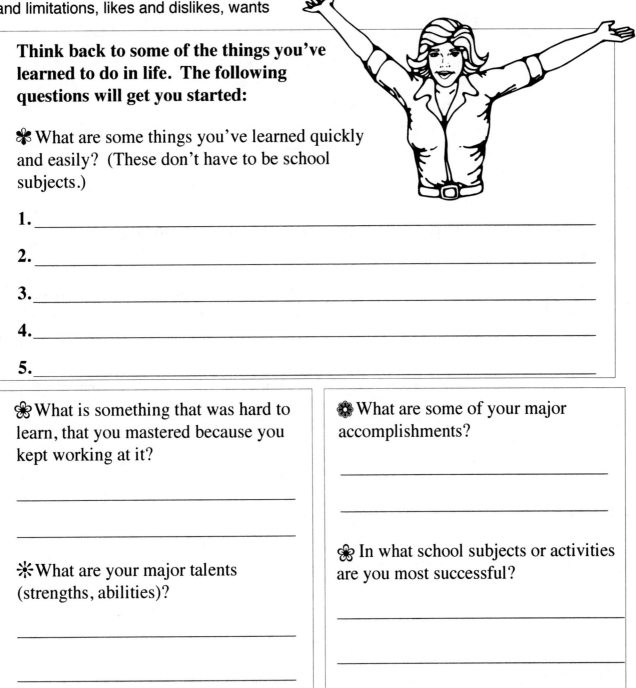

Think back to some of the things you've learned to do in life. The following questions will get you started:

❁ What are some things you've learned quickly and easily? (These don't have to be school subjects.)

1. _____

2. _____

3. _____

4. _____

5. _____

❁ What is something that was hard to learn, that you mastered because you kept working at it?

_____

_____

❁ What are your major talents (strengths, abilities)?

_____

_____

❁ What are some of your major accomplishments?

_____

_____

❁ In what school subjects or activities are you most successful?

_____

_____

What about weaknesses?

First of all, everybody's got 'em. You aren't alone. Now that you've looked at some of your strengths, let's turn the coin over and look at some of the things that students say they sometimes have trouble with. If any of these apply to you, just put a ✔ next to the item:

___ 1. Using my time well
___ 2. Standing up for myself in a situation in which I know I am right
___ 3. Overcoming shyness
___ 4. Building self-confidence
___ 5. Giving myself credit for past achievements
___ 6. Giving myself credit for present strengths
___ 7. Learning from my mistakes
___ 8. Acknowledging my present weaknesses
___ 9. Starting a conversation with a member of the opposite sex

Examine yourself closely, and complete as many of the following items as you can:

My personal strengths (talents, accomplishments, favorite activities, etc.):

1. _____

2. _____

3. _____

4. _____

5. _____

6. _____

7. _____

My personal weaknesses (difficulties, limitations, things I don't know how to do yet, etc.):

1. _____

2. _____

3. _____

4. _____

5. _____

6. _____

7. _____

If you are having trouble identifying strengths and/or weaknesses, look more closely at what has happened to you during the past week or so.

What event or activity was a high point for you?

_____

_____

What was a low point?

_____

_____

Name one person you really enjoy being with:

_____

Describe something you've experienced lately (not necessarily last week) that you hope will never happen again:

_____

_____

_____

Look back at what you've written. If you spot any clues to strengths and weaknesses you haven't thought of before, add them to your lists.

Now, complete the following half-sentences. Don't worry about being scrupulously honest or making perfect sense. Just have a good time looking at you.

I am a person who...

_____

Something I wish others could know about me is...

_____

_____

One of the things I feel proud of is...

_____

It's hard for me to admit that...

_____

One of the nicest things I could say about myself right now is...

_____

_____

A thing I accept in myself is...

_____

_____

19

A thing I can't accept in others is...

_____

One thing that makes me angry is...

_____

The best thing about being a child was...

_____

a difficult thing about being male or female is...

_____

_____

A good thing about being male or female is...

_____

_____

The way I most need to improve is...

_____

When I feel my own energy flowing through me, I...

_____

When I give myself the right to enjoy life, I...

_____

_____

One of the things I truly like and respect about myself is...

_____

I am happy when...

_____

I become angry when...

_____

I am sad when...

_____

I am fearful when...

_____

I feel lonely when...

_____

I have peace of mind when...

_____

I become frustrated when...

_____

I hate it when...

_____

I love it when...

_____

I get excited when...

_____

Admirable Qualities

List the ten qualities (such as honesty, bravery, helpfulness) you most admire in people.

1. _____

2. _____

3. _____

4. _____

5. _____

6. _____

7. _____

8. _____

9. _____

10. _____

How many of the qualities you listed do your friends have? How many do you have? What does that mean to you?

Society's Values

List ten ideals, beliefs, or values that you think all people should have. Then mark the scales below to indicate how highly you think these items are valued by society, by students at your school, and by you.

Values

1. _____

2. _____

3. _____

4. _____

5. _____

6. _____

7. _____

8. _____

9. _____

10. _____

	Low	Average	High
American Society →			
Your School →			
You →			

Stop and think about how you are expressing your values the next time you express an opinion, choose a movie or TV program, spend time on Facebook or the internet, or buy something.

The Me's I Am and Have Been
Dyad Sequence and Discussion

Objectives:

The students will:
— define themselves by describing past and present beliefs, values, abilities, disabilities, and experiences.
— demonstrate awareness that other people are also composed of many parts, including past and present abilities and disabilities.

Materials:

chairs or comfortable seating space; stop watch (or watch/clock with second hand or digital face)

Directions:

Ask the students to choose partners, forming dyads. Explain: *Sit close to and facing each other. Decide who will speak first. That person will be A, and the other person will be B. I am going to give you some topics to talk about in your dyad. First, A will talk to the topic while B Listens for one minute. Then B will talk to the same topic while A listens.*

Announce the first topic and signal the A's to commence talking. At the end of 1 minute, signal the B's to take their turn to talk. Repeat the process for the remainder of the topics.

Dyad topics:

"When I was seven years old, I liked to . . ." "When I was seven, I believed . . ."
"When I was ten, I was able to . . ."   "When I was ten, I was unable to . . ."
"Who I am now is . . ."   "One of my abilities now is . . ."
"A challenge I am currently facing is . . ." "Something I like about you is . . ."

After the students have discussed all the topics, lead a brief culminating discussion with the class.

Discussion Questions:

1. *In what ways were you and your partner similar when you were younger? How are you similar today?*

2. *How is the person you used to be as a child still part of you now?*

3. *What was one of the most interesting things you learned about your partner? What did you learn about yourself?*

4. *Can you identify how your younger self has helped to make you the person you are today?*

Thoughts, Feelings, and Behaviors
Experience Sheet and Discussion

Objectives:

The students will:
— differentiate between thoughts, feelings, and behaviors.
— state that negative feelings are triggered by negative thoughts.

Materials:

index cards labeled with thought, feeling, or behavior words listed below; the experience sheet, "The Effects of Feelings;" whiteboard

Directions:

Distribute two or three index cards to each student. Prepare these cards in advance by labeling them with various thought, feeling, and behavior words, as shown:

Thoughts	Feelings	Behaviors
remembering	joy	running
thinking	anger	talking
figuring	fear	dancing
forgetting	depression	playing
pondering	surprise	watching TV
reasoning	delight	kissing
questioning	worry	discussing
concentrating	loneliness	studying
calculating	apathy	arguing
projecting	curiosity	working

Talk about the differences between thoughts, feelings, and behaviors. Give a few examples and ask the group as a whole to name the category to which each belongs. Then have the students take turns reading their cards aloud, identifying the appropriate category. Continue until the students appear to have grasped the concept.

Have the students turn to the experience sheet, "The Effects of Feelings." Give them about 15 minutes to complete the sheet. Then ask them to form small groups and share what they have written. Conclude the activity with a class discussion.

Discussion Questions:

1. *How do thoughts affect feelings? How do feelings affect behavior?*

2. *When you have feelings that you can't explain, does that mean that they have nothing to do with your thoughts? Explain.*

3. *How can we control our feelings? ...our thoughts?*

The Effects of Feelings
Experience Sheet

Our feelings help us function in many ways. For example, have you ever become frightened and, because of your fear, done something to protect yourself from a real danger? If so, your feelings caused you to take positive action.

Below is a list of feeling words. Pick one or two of them, and see if you can briefly explain how that emotion affects your behavior. How does it work for you?

anger	joy	power	patience
eagerness	indecisiveness	satisfaction	love
fatigue	protectiveness	pain	hope
courage	silliness	curiosity	

_____

_____

Now take a moment to think about the emotions of self-pity, greed, jealousy, and possessiveness. **In what ways do you think those feelings affect behavior? What kinds of problems can they cause?**

_____

_____

_____

Feelings have an effect on your body. They can wound and they can heal. Feelings can get "locked in" to your body when you refuse to accept and deal with them. This is a type of stress, and when it happens, real sickness can result. **Do you remember a time when you or someone else got sick under pressure? How about a stomachache or headache just before a test?**

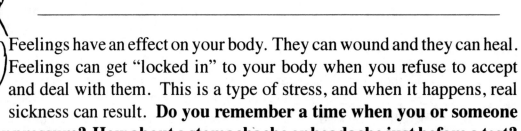

Sometimes feelings show in the form of a twitch or tic in a muscle; other times as a tight jaw or lost voice. **Below is a list of body reactions. Next to each one, list feelings that you think can lead to these body reactions.**

Tears _____

Smile _____

Lump in throat _____

Pounding heart _____

Sweaty palms _____

Clenched fists _____

Shaky arms and legs _____

Bouncy walk _____

Red face _____

Tight stomach _____

Frown _____

Squeaky voice _____

Slouched posture _____

Here are some things to try:

Get rid of old guilt feelings you may still have about something you did. The best way might be to go to the person or people you wronged, admit it, and apologize. If that isn't possible, imagine the situation. Replay it in your mind, doing what you wish you had done the first time.

Affirm yourself. People tend to like people who like themselves. You might feel ridiculous doing this, but give it a try anyway. Look in the mirror and say the nicest things you can think of to yourself *in a sincere way*. Establish a relationship with yourself as your very best friend, the person you can always count on to be on *your* side.

I Think Therefore I Feel
Experience Sheet and Discussion

Objectives:

The students will:
— describe the causal relationship between thoughts and feelings.
— state that their feelings in a situation can be improved by changing their thoughts about the situation.
— identify personal characteristics/traits that can and cannot be changed.

Materials:

the experience sheet, "Change Your Thoughts – Change Your Feelings;" whiteboard or chart paper

Directions:

On whiteboard or chart paper, make three columns. Over the first column, write the heading, "Situation." Over the second, write the heading, "Thoughts" and over the third, write the heading, "Feelings."

Begin by asking the students to help you generate a list of situations that typically lead to negative feelings. Responses might include:

- Not having a date for a big dance.
- Not knowing the answer when the teacher calls on me.
- Doing poorly on a test for which I studied hard.
- Eating lunch alone.
- Not being invited to a friend's party.
- Being eliminated during tryouts for a team, musical group, cheerleading squad, school play, etc.

List the situations in the first column. Then take one situation at a time, and ask the students what thoughts a person might be likely to have in that situation. For example, a student who has no date for an important dance might think, "I'm not fun (popular, attractive) enough." A student who doesn't know the answer to a teacher's question might think, "I always end up looking stupid." Write all suggestions in the second column.

Then go through the list and ask the students how they would feel in each situation if they had the thoughts described. For example, a person without a date who thinks she isn't any fun might feel humiliated or depressed. The person who thinks he looks stupid because he can't answer a question might feel embarrassed or frustrated. Continue making connections between the thoughts and subsequent feelings in each situation.

Suggest to the students that the feelings in each situation can be improved by changing the thoughts from negative to neutral or positive. For example, what would happen to the feelings of the student who couldn't answer his teacher's question if he thought, "I don't know the answer, but I'll listen and find out what the answer is so I'll know it next time." Make the point that situations don't cause feelings, thoughts cause feelings. No one forces a person to feel a certain way in a particular situation. **Suggest this idea: The easiest way to change your feelings about a situation is to change your thoughts about it.**

Explain that using this technique can be especially helpful when dealing with physical characteristics that are out of one's control. For example, say: *If it really bothers you that you are so tall, there's not much you can do to become shorter, but you could stop telling yourself that being tall is a curse and try focusing on your positive qualities instead.*

Pass out the experience sheet, "Change Your Thoughts – Change Your Feelings" to the students. Give the students a few minutes to write down their ideas under each example. Then have them form small groups, discuss their responses, and collectively generate additional ideas. Lead a follow-up discussion.

Discussion Questions:

1. *How do thoughts trigger feelings?*
2. *Why is it easier to change your thoughts about a situation than it is to change your feelings?*
3. *Why do we waste our time feeling miserable about things that we cannot change?*
4. *Who is in control of your thoughts? ...of your feelings?*
5. *How can understanding the power your thoughts have and how you can control them help you to be happier and successful in your future life?*

Change Your Thoughts – Change Your Feelings
Experience Sheet

We all have things about ourselves that we wish we could change, and everyone has also experienced situations which they wish had been differenet. The important thing to remember is that negative thoughts are often the causes of negative feelings and the easiest way to stop feeling badly is to chnage the thoughts you're having about it.

What could you do in each of these situations to not let negative thinking get you down? Write down your ideas:

1. Your parents are making you stay home to study for a big test, and your friends are going to the movies.

    _____

    _____

    _____

    _____

2. You are very short, and think that short people have to fight for attention and respect.

    _____

    _____

    _____

3. The medication you are taking makes your face round and full. You think you look fat and ugly.

    _____

    _____

    _____

    _____

4. You are self-conscious about your weight (too fat or too thin).

    _____

    _____

    _____

5. You think you are awkward and uncoordinated.

_____

_____

_____

_____

6. You gave a wrong answer in class and some kids laughed at you.

_____

_____

_____

7. Your best friend, with whom you hang out everyday, is moving to another town and will attend a new school.

_____

_____

_____

_____

8. You often have to hurry home after school to take care of younger brothers and sisters instead of hanging out with friends.

_____

_____

_____

_____

9. You feel shy and don't want to try to communicate with people.

_____

_____

_____

_____

10. You lost an election for student council.

_____

_____

_____

_____

Can You Hear Yourself Talk?
Experience Sheet and Discussion

Objectives:

The students will:
— define positive and negative self-talk.
— identify which style of self-talk they predominantly use.

Materials:

the experience sheet, "When You Talk to Yourself, What Do You Say?" whiteboard or chart paper

Directions:

Write the term self-talk on the board and ask the students what it means to them. Facilitate discussion, making sure to cover the following points:

- Self-talk consists of the words you say about you, either silently to yourself or audibly to another person.
- Everything you say about yourself (your self-talk) enters your subconscious mind.
- The subconscious mind believes anything you tell it, whether true or false. It makes no moral judgements; like a computer, the subconscious accepts and acts on whatever input you give it. Whatever you put in, you get back.
- When you say things about yourself that are negative, you are directing your subconscious to make you behave like a person with those same negative qualities. When you say positive things about yourself, you are directing your subconscious to make you behave in positive ways.
- Self-talk is closely related to personal effectiveness. Positive self-talk adds to your personal effectiveness. Negative self-talk robs you of effectiveness. The more positive self-talk you use, the greater your personal power, and the more control you have over your life.

Write the headings, "Positive Self-Talk" and "Negative Self-Talk" on the board. Ask the students to help you brainstorm a list of statements to write under each heading. Include statements that the students can recall making as well as statements they have heard others make. (Most likely the negative self-talk list will be longer.) Leave these lists on the board, while you have the students complete the experience sheet, "When You Talk to Yourself, What Do You Say?" When they have finished, lead a follow-up discussion.

Discussion Questions:

1. *What did you learn about yourself from taking the quiz in the experience sheet?*

2. *Why do you think our list of negative self-talk statements is longer than the list of positive statements?*

3. *How does our culture encourage negative self-talk? How does it encourage positive self-talk?*

4. *Why is it important to know what effect your self-talk can have on your well being? ... On your success in college or a career?*

5. *What specifically can you do to remind yourself to use positive self-talk?*

6. *How can learning the power of self-talk help you in your college and/or career future?*

When You Talk To Yourself, What Do You Say?
Experience Sheet

Which kind of self-talk do you mostly engage in, positive or negative? Take this quiz and find out. **Circle the answer that sounds most like the way you talk to yourself.**

1. You enter a swimming competition. You do your best, but you don't win. What do you say to yourself?
   a. *If I had only tried harder, I'd have done better.*
   b. *I did the best I could and next time I'll do better.*

2. You run for student body president, but don't win. What do you say?
   a. *I'm a loser; I never get chosen for anything.*
   b. *I did the best I could and next time I'll do even better.*

3. You have a day when everything just seems to go wrong. You tell yourself:
   a. *I really messed up everything today.*
   b. *Everybody has days like this sometimes, and I'm just not going to let it get me down.*

4. You put off doing a task you don't like until the last minute and now you're faced with a deadline. Which do you say?
   a. *I'm so lazy. I never do anything until the last minute.*
   b. *I'm getting better about not leaving things until the last minute. The next time I do this I'll have more time.*

5. You are about to take a test in your most difficult subject. What do you say?
   a. *I'm really dumb in this subject; I'm never going to pass this test.*
   b. *I've really studied for this test. I'm confident that I'll do well.*

Try this:
- For the next 3 days, pay close attention to your self-talk. Keep track of how frequently you use negative and positive self-talk.

- Make a conscious effort to use positive self-talk.

- Pay attention to the self-talk of the people around you.

- Tell others how they can use positive self-talk.

Talking to Yourself
Presentation, Discussion, and Experiment

Objectives:

The students will:
— recognize characteristics of high self-esteem and low self-esteem.
— learn and practice methods of positive self-talk.
— demonstrate understanding of how positive self-talk enhances self-esteem.

Materials:

Directions:

Ask the students if they know what is meant by the terms self-image and self-esteem. Involve the students in a discussion, making these points about the importance of self-esteem and the role of self-talk in building high self-esteem.

• Self-image is the picture you have of yourself. Self-esteem is how you feel about that picture. If you like the picture (the total person, not a photograph or image in the mirror); if it makes you feel strong, powerful, and capable, then you probably have high self-esteem. If you don't like the picture, if it makes you feel inferior, powerless, and incapable of doing things well, then you may have low self-esteem. Of course, your self-esteem can be anywhere in between, too.

• Your self-esteem significantly impacts how you behave, learn, relate, work, and play. With high self-esteem, you are poised and confident, have generally good social relationships, are less influenced by peers, and usually make good decisions. With low self-esteem, the reverse is generally true.

• Self-esteem, whether high or low, tends to be self-perpetuating. When you feel good about yourself, you project confidence and people treat you differently than they do when you feel poorly about yourself. Because you are treated well, your positive beliefs about yourself are reinforced and validated and you project even greater confidence, thus perpetuating a positive cycle. Conversely, a negative cycle occurs when you expect and project negative things about yourself. Over time, if you have high self-esteem, you:
— are proud of your accomplishments.
— tolerate frustrations as they come along.
— take responsibility for your actions.
— approach new challenges with enthusiasm.
— experience a broad range of emotions and feelings.

If you have low self-esteem, you:
— avoid situations and experiences that involve risk.
— down play or belittle your talents as not being good enough.
— blame others for your failings.
— are easily influenced by others.
— feel powerless, and are frequently defensive.
— are easily frustrated.

- Disappointments happen on a daily basis and can affect you for better or worse, depending on how you react to them. How you react is frequently based on how you feel about yourself. When you fail a test in school, if you have high self-esteem, you look at your own responsibility in the failure. You might think you could have studied more, or that next time you will pass, or that it is simply a tough subject for you. If you have low self-esteem and fail a test, you are more likely to blame the teacher or the system and to conclude that you're incapable. Your low self-esteem causes you to draw a false conclusion and verbalize it to yourself by thinking, "I must be stupid," instead of "I feel bad about failing, but it's not the worst thing that could happen. I'll do better next time." Such verbalizations are examples of SELF-TALK.

- When you were very young, one of the main ways you developed self-esteem was by paying attention to how your family, teachers, and friends treated you, and how they talked about you. If they liked you and said you were a worthwhile person, then you had good reason to feel the same way about yourself. Today, what others think and say about you is still important, but even more important is what you think about yourself, and what you say to yourself. Now that you're not a child anymore, the most powerful influence on your self-esteem is your own self-talk.

- Be watchful of your self-talk. The more positive your self-talk, the higher your self-esteem, the more negative your self-talk, the lower your self-esteem. If you find yourself saying something negative or seeing the worst possible side of a situation, tell yourself, "Stop!" Discontinue the negative thought and substitute a positive thought.

Listed below are eight situations that could lead to negative self-talk. Read each one aloud to the students, and ask volunteers to give an example of negative self-talk followed by an example of positive self-talk for each situation:

1. You strike out in a ball game.
2. You find out your parents are divorcing.
3. You get a poor grade in a class.
4. You don't make the team.
5. You are eliminated in the second round of tryouts for the cheerleading squad.
6. You lose in an election for class office.
7. When you and your best friend go places together, he or she always seems to get more attention from the opposite sex than you do.
8. You fall down during a jazz-dance recital.

Tell the students that for the next four weeks, you want them to work with a partner, consciously practicing the use of positive self-talk. Explain that the partners are to monitor, encourage, and assist each other. They are to act as an extra set of ears, calling attention to negative self-talk and reminding their partner to substitute positive self-talk. Once a week, hold a 10-minute debriefing period and ask partners to evaluate their progress.

At the end of the 4 weeks, facilitate a follow-up discussion.

Discussion Questions:

1. *How does self-talk affect self-esteem?*
2. *Why is it important to build your self-esteem?*
3. *Under what circumstances did you tend to use negative self-talk?*
4. *When did you have difficulty using positive self-talk?*
5. *What strategies did you use to help your partner? How can you use those strategies to help yourself?*

Feelings That Come with Loss
Presentation and Discussion

Objectives:

The students will:
— identify major stages and emotions associated with loss.
— describe how these emotions are experienced by the affected person, as well as by family and friends.
— recognize and understand these emotions in themselves.

Materials:

whiteboard or chart paper

Directions:

Explain that an author named Elizabeth Kubler-Ross wrote a book entitled On Death and Dying. Explain that Kubler-Ross studied many dying people and their families and developed an interesting theory about the feelings that dying people and their loved ones have. Point out that these feelings have been linked to many other kinds of loss, too. Examples include loss of physical or mental ability through illness of injury; loss of a friend due to moving away; loss of a spouse through divorce, etc.

Discuss the following emotions, making notes on the whiteboard or chart paper:

Denial

When someone refuses to believe that something bad has happened or is about to happen, he or she is said to be in denial. For example, when individuals first learn that they are going to die, they often have feelings of denial. They might say things like, "There must be some mistake," or "That doctor doesn't know what she's talking about." When a person dies suddenly, family members and friends often experience the same feelings of disbelief or denial.

Isolation

When a person suffers a major loss, such as the knowledge that he or she is dying, will never walk again, or has a serious illness like Multiple Sclerosis, that person may feel very alone at times. His or her family may have similar feelings of isolation.

Anger

It is normal to feel angry when you lose something. A person with a disability has lost one or more physical or mental abilities—sight, hearing, movement, memory, etc. A person who is seriously ill faces the loss of his or her life. During this stage, such a person might lash out at family, friends, or medical staff. Or the person could feel resentful, asking, "Why me?"

Bargaining

People who are dying sometimes try to "strike deals" to gain more time. They may say to themselves or to God, "I promise never to hurt another living soul if you'll just let me get well." Family and friends may also try to bargain.

Depression

When a person experiences a loss, he or she may develop a deep and lasting feeling of sadness. A person who is seriously ill or becomes disabled may experience physical pain, as well as a loss of material goods, self-sufficiency, and self-esteem. These losses can add up to depression, both for the person experiencing the loss and for the people around him or her.

Acceptance

When a person finally comes to terms with his or her loss, the stage of acceptance has been reached. In some situations, acceptance may not be possible.

Emphasize that these emotions may occur and reoccur throughout the process of loss or dying. People react to challenges of this nature quite differently, and responses cannot be expected to follow an orderly, prescribed sequence. Discuss how knowing about these emotions might help a person deal with loss. Invite volunteers to talk briefly about their own experiences with loss.

Discussion Questions:

1. *Do you know anyone who might have denied that he or she had a serious illness or that there was a serious illness in the family?*

2. *Have you ever tried to deny that something bad was about to happen (e.g., you had to move to a new town, were getting a bad grade, or were near a breakup in an important relationship)?*

3. *Have you ever tried to comfort someone who was experiencing a loss? What did you do or say?*

4. *Have you ever felt isolated? What did you do to feel better?*

5. *Have you ever felt angry because you were about to lose someone or something? How did you express your anger?*

6. *Have you ever tried to make a bargain to keep something bad from happening? What was the result?*

7. *How can you help someone who is depressed over a loss? What can you do to help yourself if you feel depressed?*

Coping with Anger
Experience Sheet and Discussion

Objectives:

The students will:
— learn and practice acceptable ways to express negative emotions.
— identify feelings that typically precede/precipitate anger and discuss ways of dealing with them.

Materials:

the experience sheet, "Getting Anger Under Control;" whiteboard or chart paper

Directions:

Write the heading, "Anger" on the board. Ask the class to brainstorm specific examples of angry behavior and list them beneath the heading. Then read the following scenario to the class:

Laura is a bright girl and an average student. She blames her mother for the her parents' recent divorce and for the fact that she rarely sees her father, whom she misses. Laura's mother works long hours and frequently doesn't get home until 7 p.m. or later. Laura's grades are dropping and she has been hanging out with some kids who use drugs. Today, Laura comes to math class unprepared. Throughout most of the class, she talks and tries to antagonize other students, which thoroughly frustrates the teacher. In addition, Laura sarcastically criticizes the previous day's homework assignment, which she found extremely difficult and failed to complete. After speaking to Laura a number of times, the teacher finally writes a referral and sends her to the office for discipline. At first Laura is surprised and tries to talk her way out of the referral. The teacher will have none of it. By the time she gets to the office, Laura is seething. She is rude to the secretary, blames the teacher for her upset, and threatens to quit school. Later that day, she finds the teacher's car and scratches the paint on one side. Then she heads for the park to meet her friends and share a joint.

Following the story, facilitate discussion by asking these questions:

—*What do you think is going on with Laura?*

—*Why did she criticize the homework assignment?*

—*What were her first emotions when the teacher handed her the referral?*

—*Could she have expressed those emotions? If so, how? If not, why not?*

—*Why did Laura scratch her teacher's car?*

—*Why do you think Laura is using drugs?*

—*What actions could help Laura get control of her life before things get even worse?*

Make the following points in a discussion about anger:

- Anger is a normal emotion. We all get angry and need to learn acceptable and effective ways to deal with anger.
- Anger tends to be a secondary emotion. In other words, one or more other feelings usually precede anger. For example, when Laura found herself facing a referral, her first emotions were surprise and shock. Next, she may have felt humiliation, panic, regret, and desperation in rapid succession. She tried unsuccessfully to defend herself. Her efforts frustrated, Laura headed for the office with anger building inside her.
- When a teenager comes home very late from a date, a worried parent erupts almost immediately in anger, but the first feeling—the unexpressed feeling—is relief. "Thank heavens, you're okay."
- When a student fails a test for which she or he studied many long hours, the first feelings are overwhelming disappointment and frustration. But anger may follow so quickly it's the only emotion the rest of the class observes.
- Other people usually have difficulty coping with someone's anger. This is partly because anger acts as a mask, hiding what is really going on. Others will have a much easier time responding to your frustration, grief, relief, sadness, or fear than to your anger. Consequently, a very valuable skill to develop is the skill of expressing your initial feelings, rather than just your anger.
- Anger puts stress on the body and can lead to illness.

Pass out the experience sheet, "Getting Anger Under Control" to each student. Go over the directions and give the students a few minutes to read the three situations described. Then have the students form small groups. Direct the groups to discuss the situations and brainstorm answers to the questions, recording ideas on their individual sheets. When the groups have finished, lead a culminating class discussion.

Discussion Questions:

1. *What did you decide were Mark's first emotions? ...Jennifer's? ...Sam's?*
2. *How could each character have expressed his or her first emotions?*
3. *What other alternative behaviors did you come up with in each situation?*
4. *How does anger mask what is really going on?*
5. *Why is anger such a difficult emotion to deal with in other people?*
6. *If you have difficulty dealing with anger, what can you do to get help?*
7. *Why is the ability to manage your anger a benefit throughout life in all situations?*

Getting Anger Under Control
Experience Sheet

Anger is a normal but difficult emotion. Our anger often comes up in response to some other feeling — like hurt, worry, embarrassment, jealousy, or frustration. Knowing the feeling that caused our anger can make the anger itself easier to control. Read the situations below and see if you can empathize with Mark, Jennifer, and Sam enough to understand the emotions that led to their anger. Then brainstorm three alternative behaviors that would have achieved better results in each situation.

Situation 1: During a varsity baseball game, Mark ignores the base coach's signal and races for third base. As he slides into base the umpire calls him out. Mark immediately argues and makes rude remarks about the umpire's ability to see and judge the play. He continues his remarks as he moves toward the dugout. He kicks dirt, says things to the opposing team, and makes a gesture to the umpire who then kicks him out of the game. After he leaves the field, he shouts more angry remarks.

What were Mark's first feelings after he realized his mistake?

1. _____

   _____

2. _____

   _____

How could he have expressed those feelings in a more positive way?

1. _____

   _____

2. _____

   _____

3. _____

   _____

40

Situation 2: Jennifer works at a fast food restaurant. She does not like working the drive-thru window but is often assigned that task. Two of her responsibilities are to ask the customers if they want drinks with their order and to offer new items on the menu. Jennifer tends to ignore that part of the job because the pressure is usually so intense that she can barely get the orders filled. Her manager has spoken to her before about the necessity of following these procedures. Today, Jennifer is more harried than usual and doesn't offer the new items or ask about drinks. On her break, the manager talks to her and tells her she must improve in this area or she will be fired. Jennifer glares at the manager, tenses her body, and grumbles, "If they want it, they'll order it. I shouldn't have to ask." The manager says it is part of the job. Jennifer cries, "You're never satisfied. I can't do anything right. I quit!"

What were Jennifer's first feelings when her manager confronted her?

1. _____

_____

2. _____

_____

How could she have expressed those feelings in a more positive way?

1. _____

_____

2. _____

_____

3. _____

_____

Situation 3: At home, Sam has been told repeatedly to clean his room. Frankly, it's become such a terrible mess that he doesn't know where to start. Besides, part of the reason it's a mess is that his older brother, who has gone off to college, is still taking up half the closet space. Today his mother has insisted that he will not go out with his friends again until his room is clean. Sam slams his bedroom door hard, takes a kick at the door leaving black scuff marks on it, and then makes a fist and punches a major hole in the wall. He lies down, lights up a cigarette, and plans how he will wait until his mother is busy and then go out to meet his friends anyway.

What were Sam's first feelings after his mother threatened to ground him?

1. _____

_____

2. _____

_____

How could he have expressed those feelings in a more positive way?

1. _____

_____

2. _____

_____

3. _____

_____

Success Bombardment
Experience Sheet and Group Exercise

Objectives:

The students will:
— recognize and describe their own worth and worthiness.
— identify strengths, talents, and special abilities in themselves and others.
— practice positive self-talk.

Note: For optimum impact, use this activity after your students have had time to develop as a group, e.g., have experienced several activities and Sharing Circles together.

Materials:

the experience sheet, "Success Inventory;" 12 small self-adhesive labels per student; and 1 copy of the "Target" worksheet for each student

Directions:

Pass out the experience sheet, "Success Inventory (2 pages)" to each student. Go over the directions and answer any questions. Have the students work individually to fill out the sheets. If the students appear to be having trouble thinking of accomplishments, take a couple of minutes and talk to the entire class about such examples as learning to walk, talk, dress, dance, play, sing, count, problem-solve, read, write, love, ride a bike, skateboard, roller-skate, ski, play softball, volleyball, soccer, basketball, cook, play an instrument, use a computer, be a friend, join an organization, earn a merit badge, award, or certificate; learn to type, baby-sit, drive a car, care for a pet, etc., etc. Explain that these are all accomplishments.

When the students have completed their sheets, ask them to form groups of four or five. Give 12 small, blank, self-adhesive labels and a "Target" worksheet to each student.

Direct the students to take turns describing their accomplishments to the other members of their group. In your own words, explain: *Tell your group why you picked those particular successes. Explain how you felt about them at the time they occurred and why they are particularly meaningful to you now. Immediately after you share, the other members of your group will each make three labels that describe positive things about you based on the successes you shared. For example, the first person's labels might say, "industrious and energetic," "musically talented," and "born to lead." Then, while you hold up your "target," that person will look directly at you, tell you what he or she has written on each label, and stick the labels on your target. The other members of your group will then take a turn "bombarding" you with their success labels in the same manner. If there are three other people in your group (total of four), you will end up with nine labels on your target. A second person in the group will then take a turn reading his or her successes and being "bombarded." Then a third person will be the target, and so on until everyone in your group has been 'bombarded' by everyone else in the group.*

Circulate and assist the groups, as needed. Although the students are expected to enjoy the exercise, make sure that they appreciate its seriousness and do not engage in any kind of teasing or put-downs. If you observe any student using the third person ("She is industrious and energetic.") when labeling a "target," stop the person and help him or her rephrase the statement in the second person. ("You are industrious and energetic.") Lead a follow-up discussion.

Discussion Questions:

1. *How do you feel after doing this exercise?*
2. *What did you learn about yourself? ...about other members of your group?*
3. *How did you decide which accomplishments to include on your list?*
4. *Why do you suppose we spend so much time thinking about our failures and deficiencies when we have all accomplished so much?*
5. *Where can you put your target so that it will continue to remind you of your successes?*

Success Inventory
Experience Sheet

Your life is a chronicle of successes, one after another, year after year. The things you've accomplished could fill a book. Look back now at the child you were and the young adult you have become. Recall some of the many things you've learned and achieved, and write the most memorable here:

Five skills I mastered before the age of 5 were:

1. _____

2. _____

3. _____

4. _____

5. _____

Four things I accomplished between the ages of 5 and 8 were:

1. _____

2. _____

3. _____

4. _____

Four of my achievements between the ages of 8 and 11 were:

1._____

_____

2._____

_____

3._____

_____

4._____

_____

Three major things I accomplished between the ages of 11 and 13 were:

1._____

_____

2._____

_____

3._____

_____

✴ ✴ ✴

Three of my successes between the age of 13 and now are:

1._____

_____

2._____

_____

3._____

_____

TARGET
Worksheet

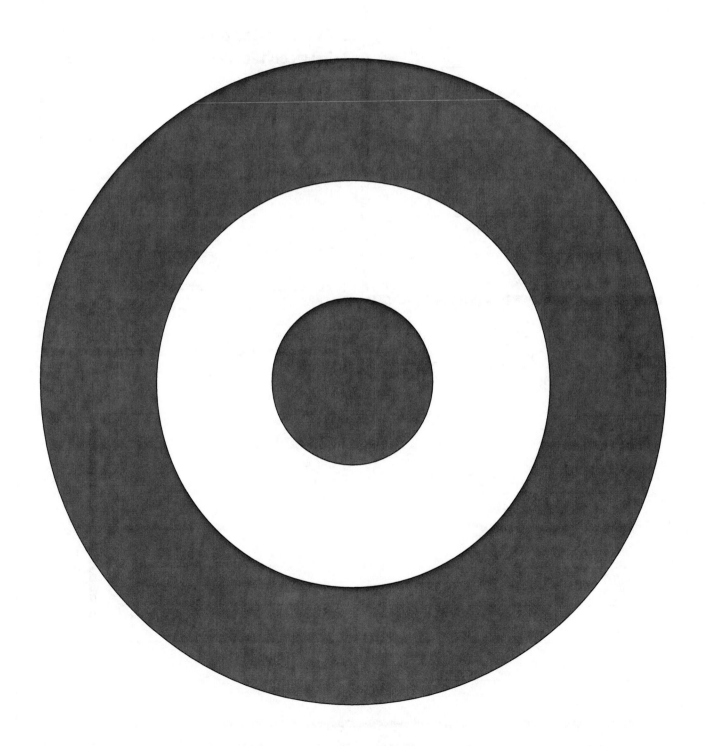

When I Feel Comfortable Just Being Me
A Sharing Circle

Objectives:

The students will:
— recognize and describe their own worth and worthiness.

Introduce the Topic:

One of the ways that we create stress in our lives is by trying to change ourselves to please other people. We think we aren't attractive enough, or smart enough, or athletic enough, or we decide that the events in our life aren't exciting enough. Our dissatisfaction causes us to indulge in negative self-talk which is both psychologically damaging and stressful. So today, we're going to talk about circumstances that cause us to feel satisfied with ourselves just the way we are. Our topic is, "When I Feel Comfortable Just Being Me."

Think of a time recently when you felt totally acceptable just the way you are. Who were you with? What were you doing? Maybe you're comfortable with yourself in the company of a particular friend, someone who likes you just the way you are. Or maybe you experience this kind of comfort when you're engaged in a favorite hobby, or physical or mental activity. Or perhaps you feel comfortable with yourself just the way you are when you accomplish something that you didn't realize you could do. Think about it for a few moments. The topic is, "When I Feel Comfortable Just Being Me."

Discussion Questions:

1. *What did you learn about yourself from this session?*

2. *How can you use this information to reduce stress in your life?*

3. *What attitudes and behaviors on the part of others help us feel comfortable with ourselves and our abilities? ...our disabilities?*

4. *Who creates self-dissatisfaction? Who can eliminate it?*

5. *Why is it important to be comfortable with yourself in all aspects of your life?*

I Did Something Impulsive
and Regretted It Later
A Sharing Circle

Objectives:

The students will:
— describe instances of impulsive behavior and what caused them.
— identify specific consequences of impulsive behaviors.
— discuss strategies for controlling impulses.

Introduce the Topic:

Our topic today is, "I Did Something Impulsive and Regretted It Later." Think of a time when you did something on the spur of the moment—something that you probably would not have done if you had waited a while. Maybe you bought something that you didn't really need, or couldn't afford. Or maybe on the spur of the moment you decided to go with some friends who later ended up doing something dangerous or illegal. Perhaps you had a sudden impulse to take something that didn't belong to you, say something hurtful to another person, or copy off of someone else's paper. Whatever it was, you were sorry later. If you decide to share, describe to us not only the impulsive thing that you did, but why you regretted doing it. Take a few moments to think about it. The topic is, "I Did Something Impulsive and Regretted It Later."

Discussion Questions:

1. *What does the word "impulsive" mean?*

2. *Why do we sometimes do impulsive things?*

3. *What causes us to regret many of the things we do on impulse?*

4. *What are some ways that we can better control our impulses?*

A Time I Really Controlled Myself
A Sharing Circle

Objectives:

The students will:
— describe a time when they exercised self-control.
— identify acceptable ways to express negative emotions.

Introduce the Topic:

Most of us occasionally have a hard time controlling our emotions, particularly when we are angry, disappointed, or excited. This can be especially true if we have developed a habit of reacting in a particular way—for example, reacting defensively when we are criticized. Today, however, we're going to talk about times when we overcame all those impulses and habits and stayed in very good control. Our topic is, "A Time I Really Controlled Myself."

Think of a time when you were able to control your behavior even though your feelings were pretty strong. Perhaps you had just heard some exciting news and wanted to tell your best friend, but he or she was in a very bad mood, so you decided to contain your excitement till later. Maybe someone made you very angry but you didn't want to get into trouble by fighting so you held your tongue and walked away. Or maybe a person said something that hurt you a great deal and you felt like crying, but didn't want to give the person the satisfaction of knowing how badly you felt. Think of a time like this when you had to exercise great control. The topic is, "A Time I Really Controlled Myself."

Discussion Questions:

1. *What were the similarities in everyone's experiences? What were the differences?*

2. *Why is it sometimes difficult to hold back our feelings?*

3. *What would it be like if all people were unable to control their feelings?*

4. *What are some healthy ways of controlling or expressing anger? ...jealousy? ...fear?*

SOCIAL SKILLS AND FRIENDSHIP

Social skills, vital to developing and maintaining healthy relationships, consist of effective listening, observing, and communicating. Through listening, students gather information, develop working relationships, foster intergroup harmony, and build trust. Skillful listening is required for facilitating discussions, negotiating agreements, mediating conflicts, and many other responsibilities of college and career life. Leaders in all areas need to use verbal and nonverbal communication to articulate ideas, give directions, paint visions, and motivate constituents. Effective use of language requires more than grammar and vocabulary skills. The use of "I" messages allows a leader to be assertive, while promoting understanding and preserving harmony.

Friendship and healthy relationships are enhanced by positive social skills. This unit also gives students opportunities to examine the elements and dynamics of friendship. Through structured experiences and discussions, they identify qualities they admire and ingredients they desire in friends, and they assess their own friendship skills while developing their abilities to build a wide range of friendly relationships.

Play It Back! Like a Tape Recorder
A Listening Activity

Objectives:

The students will:
— demonstrate attentive listening with a series of partners.
— state how they let others know they are listening.

Materials:

Directions:

Assign the students to groups of eight or ten. (An even number in each group is essential for this activity to work. If a group is one short, join that group during the activity.)

Ask the students to choose a partner. Explain that both people will take turns speaking to the same topic. As the first person (A) speaks for 1 minute, the second person (B) must listen very carefully, gathering information very much like a tape recorder. The listener should not interrupt or ask questions, except for clarification. When time is called, B will have 1 minute to "playback" to A as accurately as possible what he or she heard. Then A and B will switch roles. B will become the speaker and talk about the same topic for 1 minute while A listens. Then A will have 1 minute to "playback" what she or he heard. This will complete the first round, and the students will find new partners within their group.

Signal the end of each minute and give clear instructions. Conduct enough rounds so that every person is paired once with every other person in his or her group. (For example, if groups contain eight students, conduct seven rounds.)

Suggested topics:

"My Favorite Hobby or Pastime"
"My Favorite TV Show or Movie"
"My Favorite Game or Sport"
"My Favorite Song or Musical Group"
"Something I Want To Do This Weekend"
"Something I Want To Do After I Finish
          High School"

"My Favorite Food"
"My Favorite Animal"
"Something That Makes Me Happy"
"Something I'm Looking Forward To"
"My Favorite Story, Poem, Book, or
          Magazine"

Discussion Questions:

1. *How did you feel as the speaker during this exercise?*

2. *How did you feel as the listener?*

3. *What was hardest about listening like a voice recorder?*

4. *Did speaking and/or listening get harder or easier as you went from partner to partner?*

5. *Of what value is silent, attentive listening to effective communication? Why is it a good idea to "play back" what you hear?*

6. *What are some things you can do to show someone that you are really listening?*

7. *How can knowing how to be a good listener help you in college? in a job?*

The Active Listener
Communication Skill Practice

Objectives:

The students will:
— define the role of the receiver in communication.
— identify and demonstrate "active listening" behaviors.

Materials:

a diagrammatic model of the communications process (see below) drawn on the whiteboard or chart paper; a list of topics written on the whiteboard (see below); the "Active Listening" experience sheet

Procedure:

On the whiteboard or chart paper, draw a simple diagram illustrating the communication process. For example, print the words, SENDER and RECEIVER and draw two arrows—one going in each direction—between the two words.

SENDER  RECEIVER

Explain to the students that in order for two people to enjoy and encourage each other, to work, play, or solve problems together, they need to be able to communicate effectively. In your own words, say: *In every example of communication, no matter how small, a message is sent from one person (the sender) to the other person (the receiver). The message is supposed to tell the receiver something about the feelings and/or thoughts of the sender. Because the sender cannot "give" the receiver his or her feelings and thoughts, they have to be "coded" in words. Good communicators pick words that describe their feelings and thoughts as closely as possible. Nonverbal "signals" almost always accompany the verbal message; for example, a smile, a frown, or a hand gesture. Sometimes the entire message is nonverbal. Good communicators send nonverbal signals that exactly match their feelings and thoughts.*

Ask the students to describe what a good receiver says and does to show that he or she is interested in what the sender is saying and is really listening. Write their ideas on the board. Be sure to include these behaviors:

1. Face the sender.
2. Look into the sender's eyes.
3. Be relaxed, but attentive.
4. Listen to the words and try to picture in your own mind what the sender is telling you.
5. Don't interrupt or fidget. When it is your turn to respond, don't change the subject or start telling your own story.

6. If you don't understand something, wait for the sender to pause and then ask, "What do you mean by..."
7. Try to feel what the sender is feeling (show empathy).
8. Respond in ways that let the sender know that you are listening and understand what is being said. Ways of responding might include nodding, saying "uh huh," or giving feedback that proves you are listening, for example:
   • Briefly summarize: "You're saying that you might have to quit the team in order to have time for a job."
   • Restate feelings: "You must be feeling pretty bad." or "You sound really happy!"

Tell the students that this type of listening is called active listening. Ask them if they can explain why the word active is used to describe it.

Ask the students to form groups of three. Tell them to decide who is A, who is B, and who is C. Announce that you are going to give the students an opportunity to practice active listening. Explain the process: *In the first round, A will be the sender and B will be the receiver and will use active listening. C will be the observer. C's job is to notice how well B listens, and report his/her observations at the end of the round. I will be the timekeeper. We will have three rounds, so that you can each have a turn in all three roles. When you are the sender, pick a topic from the list on the board, and remember to pause occasionally so that your partner can respond.*

Signal the start of the first round. Call time after 3 minutes. Have the observers give feedback for 1 minute. Tell the students to switch roles. Conduct two more rounds. Lead a follow-up discussion. As a reinforcement, at the conclusion of the activity have the students complete their experience sheets.

Discussion Questions:

1. *How did it feel to "active listen?"*
2. *What was it like to be the observer?*
3. *When you were the sender, how did you feel having someone really listen to you?*
4. *What was easiest about active listening? What was hardest?*
5. *What did you learn from your observer?*
6. *Why is it important to learn to be a good listener?*
7. *Why is it important for leaders to be good listeners?*

List of topics:

"A Time I Needed Some Help"
"A Problem I Need to Solve"
"A Time I Made a Tough Decision"

"Something I'd Like to Do Better"
"A Time I Got Into an Argument"
"Something I'd Like to Be or Do When I'm an Adult"

Active Listening
Experience Sheet

In order for two or more people to live, to work, to play, or to work on a problem together they need to be able to communicate effectively. Listening is a very important part of good communication. Listed below are characteristics of a good listener. Check ones that describe you most of the time.

A good listener:

____ Faces the speaker.

____ Looks into the speaker's eyes.

____ Is relaxed, but attentive.

____ keeps an open mind.

____ Listens to the words and tries to picture what the speaker is saying.

____ Doesn't interrupt or fidget.

____ Waits for the sender to pause to ask clarifying questions.

____ Tries to feel what the sender is feeling (shows empathy).

____ Nods and says "uh huh," or summarizes to let the speaker know he or she is listening.

What is your strongest quality as a listener?

_____

_____

_____

What is your weakest quality as a listener?

_____

_____

_____

How can you become a better listener?

_____

_____

_____

Follow My Lead
Group Experiment and Discussion

Objectives:

The students will:
— use precise verbal and nonverbal communication to lead a partner to a hidden object.
— describe the importance of precise communication.
— state why effective communication is vital to leadership.

Materials:

a large open area, as free as possible of physical obstacles; scarves, large handkerchiefs, or strips of opaque fabric to use as blindfolds

Directions:

Note: You may wish to conduct the second round of this activity in a series of three to five 3-minute segments. This will limit the number of pairs on the floor at any given time, diminishing sound interference and increasing safety.

Begin the activity by talking briefly about the need for clarity, accuracy, and conciseness in communication. Announce that the students are going to participate in an activity that will test their ability to communicate with clarity.

Have the students choose partners and decide who will be the Leader in the first round. Then, in your own words, explain: When you are the Leader, you are going to use clear, precise verbal communication to guide your partner, who will be blindfolded, to an object hidden somewhere in the room. You must use as few directions as possible, so pick your words carefully. Stay close to your partner, talking quietly but distinctly, but DO NOT touch your partner. Blindfolded partners may ask questions for clarification. Remember that other pairs will be moving about the room, and it is your responsibility as the leader to prevent collisions. At the end of 3 minutes, I'll call time and you will switch roles for the second round.

Together, have each pair pick an object (book, key, pen, backpack, etc.) to be "found" during the activity. Instruct the Leaders to blindfold their partners. Then give the Leaders 1 minute to hide their object somewhere in the room.

Allow about 3 minutes for the Leaders to verbally guide their partners to the hidden objects. Then gather the class together and give these instructions for the second round: The goal of the Leader is the same in the second round—to lead your blindfolded partner to a hidden object. However, you must do the guiding nonverbally.

You MAY NOT touch your partner, but you will have 2 minutes before the round to agree on a series of signals for various movements, such as Left, Right, Stop, Up, Down, etc. You may use claps, snaps, stomps, taps or any other clear signal that you can invent. Blindfolded partners may ask questions for clarification; however, Leaders may not answer in words.

Have the partners pick a second object. Allow 2 minutes for signal planning. Then have the Leaders blindfold their partners and hide the object. Allow 3 minutes for the Leaders to guide their partner to the object. Conclude the activity with a class discussion.

Discussion Questions:

1. *What was it like to be the Leader in round one? ...in round two?*

2. *How did you feel when you were the partner being led?*

3. *How successfully did you communicate as a Leader?*

4. *What were some of the problems you encountered and how did you solve them?*

5. *What did you learn about communication from this activity?*

6. *What did you learn about leadership?*

7. *Why would being able to communicate clearly and precisely be a valuable skill in college? ...in a job?*

Making Friends
Class Discussion and Experience Sheet

Objectives:

The students will:
— describe positive and negative qualities of friendships.
— discuss how to make and keep friends.
— describe the benefits of developing diversity in friendships.

Materials:

the experience sheet, "What Is a Friend?"; whiteboard or chart paper and markers

Directions:

On the board or chart paper, write the heading, "Friendships." Beneath that heading, write the subheadings "Positive" and "Negative."

Lead an introductory discussion on the subject of friendship. Begin by pointing out that although friendships are usually positive, the roots of some friendships are negative. Elaborate on the notion that positive friendships are based on such things as common interests; mutual acceptance, trust, and respect; interdependence, sharing, and cooperation. Negative friendships are based on unhealthy things, such as dominance, dependence, fear, low self esteem, and unmet needs for attention, acceptance, and affection.

Ask the students to name and discuss positive reasons for choosing a friend, such as, "We both like to hike." List their reasons under the appropriate heading. (You may want to provide the first one or two examples.) Then list and discuss several examples of negative reasons, such as "If I'm her friend, she'll drive me to school in her car." At the conclusion of the discussion, distribute the experience sheet, "What Is a Friend?" Give the students a few minutes to complete the experience sheet. Allow talking/interaction during the work period. When the students have completed their experience sheets, lead a culminating discussion.

Discussion Questions:

1. *Why do you think people stay in negative friendships?*
2. *Why do you think it's important to have positive friendships?*
3. *Is it harder for a person with a disability to make friends? Why?*
4. *What are the benefits of choosing friends who are different from you with respect to background? ... culture? ... interests? ... values? ... ableness?*

What Is a Friend?
Experience Sheet

1. ____YES ___NO   A friend is someone who knows all about me and likes me as I am.

2. ____YES ___NO   To be my friend, a person must agree with me on just about every subject or issue.

3. ____YES ___NO   A friend is someone who doesn't care how much money I have.

4. ____YES ___NO   To be my friend, a person must have the same racial, cultural, and religious background as I.

5. ____YES ___NO   A friend is someone who'll do whatever I say.

6. ____YES ___NO   A friend is someone who listens to me even if I am talking about my troubles.

7. ____YES ___NO   To be my friend, a person must demonstrate respect for me.

If you said "YES" to numbers 1, 3, 6, and 7, you have probably had some real friends. Your friends know and like you because of the person you are, which includes the color or your skin, the way you speak, how much money you have, your abilities, and your disabilities. They care how you feel. They listen to your thoughts and feelings. That's how they prove that they are friends. If you answered "NO" to numbers 2, 4, and 5, you realize that everybody's different and that's great. Friends don't have to look alike, talk the same way, come from the same background, or agree with each other all of the time. And they don't always have to do what each other wants to prove their friendship.

Think of a friend you had when you were a child:

What did you like about your friend?

_____

_____

What do you think he or she liked about you?

_____

_____

What was one of the best times you ever had together?

_____

_____

Think about someone who is your friend now:

How did your friendship begin?

_____

_____

_____

_____

What are some things you like to do together?

_____

_____

_____

_____

How is your friendship different now from the way if was in the beginning?

_____

_____

_____

_____

Have you ever had a friendship that seemed bad for you? What was it about that friendship that was negative?

_____

_____

_____

_____

List the most important things you want in a friend.

1. _____

_____

2. _____

_____

3. _____

_____

4. _____

_____

5. _____

_____

6. _____

_____

Other things to think about:

❋ What do you think you would do if you wanted to be friends with someone who spoke a different language?

❋ What do you think you'd do if a friend of yours started doing something you thought was wrong or dangerous?

❋ How could you make friends with someone who is blind? ...someone who is deaf?

Setting Friendship Goals
Experience Sheet and Dyad Sharing

Objectives:

The students will:
— identify what they and others like and don't like about their own friendship behaviors.
— identify ways to decrease negative friendship behaviors and increase positive ones.
— formulate a goal and plan for improving one friendship behavior.

Materials:

the experience sheet, "Becoming a Better Friend"; whiteboard or chart paper

Directions:

Begin by reminding the students of previous discussions/assignments concerning friendship. Announce that today the students are going to concentrate on evaluating their own friendship behaviors.

Ask several volunteers to name things they could begin doing (or stop doing) that would make them a better friend. List ideas on the board, such as:

- Pay attention when in a conversation with others.
- Volunteer to help someone study for a test.
- Reach out to someone of a different race or cultural background.
- Invite someone to eat lunch with you.
- Help a friend learn a new skill or game.
- Stick up for your friends (be loyal).
- Learn how to settle conflicts and negotiate differences.
- Practice giving compliments.
- Smile and use good eye contact when talking with others.
- Bring together friends from different groups in some common pursuit.

Ask the students to continue thinking about their own behaviors, and to name some that others respond to positively, as well as some that seem to turn others off. Offer examples from your own experience. You might say: My *positive friendship behaviors are that I always do what I say I'm going to do, so my friends can count on me. In addition, I have a generally positive attitude. I smile a lot, and I try to remember to tell people when I like their work, or something they've done, or the way they look. A negative behavior I need to work on is letting my thoughts jump ahead during conversations, because when I jump ahead, I tend to interrupt the person who is speaking.*

Continue taking examples from the group until you think the students have the idea. Then pass out the experience sheet, "Becoming a Better Friend." Go over it briefly, answering any questions. Allow the students time to complete the sheet.

Have the students pair up. Instruct the partners to each share three positive behaviors and one negative behavior, as you did in your earlier example. Suggest that they select from their experience sheet those behaviors they would most like to discuss. Allow about 5 minutes for sharing, signaling the partners at the halfway point.

Get the attention of the pairs, and take a few moments to talk about the importance of goals in changing behavior. Point out that no one is born knowing how to make and keep friends; rather, these behaviors are learned. When behaviors are learned, they can also be changed. Change involves setting goals for new behaviors and implementing step by step plans for achieving those goals.

Give the partners an additional 5 to 10 minutes to share their goals and action plans. Suggest that they help each other formulate steps for achieving their goals. Urge them to make a mutual contract to support each other through continued informal sharing and discussion over the next few weeks. Lead a culminating class discussion.

Discussion Questions:

1. *How do you explain the fact that some people have so many friends and others have so few?*

2. *Why are friendships important? What do we gain from having friends?*

3. *Which was easier, naming positive friendship behaviors or naming negative friendship behaviors? Why?*

4. *What kinds of help and support do you need to really pursue your friendship goal? How and from whom will you get that help and support?*

Becoming a Better Friend
Experience Sheet

Friends are important! If you could take three people with you on a trip around the world, whom would you take? Why?

Name	Reason

1. _____

_____

2. _____

_____

3. _____

_____

Keep it growing. Do you have a friendship with someone that just keeps getting better? What have you done to keep it growing?

_____

_____

_____

_____

What do you value in your friends? Complete this statement: People can show their friendship to me by...

_____

_____

_____

_____

Name at least five of *your own* friendship behaviors that others seem to like:

1. _____

_____

2. _____

_____

3. _____

_____

4. _____

_____

5. _____

_____

_____

Name two of *your own* friendship behaviors that seem to turn others off:

1._____

_____

2._____

_____

Think of *one way* in which you would like to improve your friendship behavior. Write a GOAL here:

_____

_____

_____

_____

_____

_____

_____

To achieve your goal, you need a PLAN—a systematic way of putting your goal into action. What are some of the first steps you can take?

Step 1:_____

_____

Step 2:_____

_____

Step 3:_____

_____

Step 4:_____

_____

Step 5:_____

_____

Step 6:_____

_____

_____

The Friendship Shake
Introductions and Conversation Starters

Objectives:

The students will:
— practice making introductions.
— practice starting and maintaining conversations.

Materials:

the experience sheet, "Conversation Log" for each student; whiteboard and marker

Directions:

Announce that today the group is going to practice important friendship skills: making introductions and starting conversations. Point out that if people don't know how to make introductions or begin conversations, many opportunities to start new relationships are lost. It's not uncommon to feel a desire to know someone, yet be unsure where or how to begin.

Use the "Handshake" game to form three groups of students: Ask the students to "meditate" for a moment and SILENTLY decide on a number one, two, or three. Then direct the students to get up and SILENTLY find their numerical "partners," by mingling around and shaking hands with one another. If their number is one, they are to firmly shake each hand one time. If their number is two, they firmly shake each hand twice. If their number is three, they shake three times. Explain that when two students with different numbers shake hands, they will experience a moment of tension when one stops shaking and the other continues. But when both have the same number, they will stop shaking at the same moment and *will know* instantly that they are in the same group. They must then stick together while searching for other members of their group. (The resulting groups will probably be about the same size, but don't be concerned if they're not.)

Once the groups are formed, get everyone's attention and offer the following model for introducing oneself to another person:

1. Approach the person you want to meet.
2. Say, "Hello ... .. Hi," or offer some other greeting.
3. Say, "My name is..."
4. Wait for the person to say his or her name or ask, "What's your name?"

All together, the steps sound like this: "Hi, my name's Diana. What's your name?"

Give the students a few minutes to practice these steps with one another in their newly formed groups. Then offer this model for introducing two people to each other:

1. Look at the first person and say that person's name.
2. Tell the first person the second person's name
3. Repeat the process with the second person.

All together, the steps sound like this: "Andy, this is Lucy Becerra. Lucy, this is Andy Gilbert."

Have the students practice the steps in their groups, experiencing several rounds of introductions with different members. Then point out that a conversation frequently follows an introduction. The following steps are helpful when starting a conversation.

1. Look at the person with whom you want to speak.
2. Say something about yourself (for example, something you like).
3. Ask the person about something he or she likes.
4. Offer a positive response related to what the person says.

All together, the steps sound like this:

Person 1: "1 really enjoy aerobics and hiking. How do you stay in shape?"
Person 2: "1 like hiking too, but I'm not sure where the good trails are around here."
Person 1: "1 know some great trails. Why don't we go hiking together some Sunday?"

Have the students pair up within their groups and practice starting conversations. Remind them to switch partners every few minutes. After the students have practiced for 5 to 10 minutes, reconvene the class and pass out the "Conversation Log" experience sheets. Explain that you want them to keep track of conversations they initiate over the next week, making notes on their log. Answer any questions. Conclude the activity with a class discussion.

Discussion Questions:

1. *How did you feel when you were introducing yourself? ... when you were introducing two other people?*
2. *How did you feel when you were attempting to start a conversation?*
3. *What is the easiest part of starting a conversation? What is the hardest part?*
4. *What are some other methods of getting to know new people?*
5. *How do you feel when the person you want to talk with doesn't seem interested? What's the best thing to do in instances like that?*

Follow up:

Approximately 1 week following this activity, have the students get back together in their original groups and share highlights from their Conversation Logs.

Conversation Log
Experience Sheet

For one week, notice each time you make an introduction or start a conversation. Pay attention to what happens and how you feel. Use the chart below to record your observations, feelings, and thoughts. Later, you'll have an opportunity to share these notes with your group.

Day	Introduction/ Conversation	What I Think/Feel

How I Get People to Pay Attention to Me
A Sharing Circle

Objectives:

The students will:
— describe methods of gaining the attention of others.
— state that attending and having the attention of others are essential to good communication.

Introduce the Topic:

Today our topic is, "How I Get People to Pay Attention to Me." When you or I want to communicate with someone, first of all we have to get that person to focus on us. There are many ways to do this. For example, if you do something funny, destructive, or bizarre, people will automatically look at you. If you don't want every head in the room to turn, you have to do something less unusual. What do you do?

How do you get the attention of a family member engrossed in a TV program? What do you do to get the attention of a friend some distance from you in a large crowd? How do you capture the attention of someone two tables away in a quiet classroom or library? If you can think of a specific incident in which you used a particular method, tell us about it. The topic is, "How I Get People to Pay Attention to Me."

Discussion Questions:

1. *When do we need to capture the attention of others?*

2. *What relationship is there between the way you get attention, the kind of attention you get, and how long the attention lasts?*

3. *How do you feel when a person refuses to pay attention to you no matter what you do?*

A Time I Listened Well to Someone
A Sharing Circle

Objectives:

The students will:
— describe a time when they listened effectively.
— identify effective listening behaviors.

Introduce the Topic:

Most of us appreciate having someone really listen to us. In this session we are going to turn this idea around and talk about how it feels to listen to someone else. The topic is, "A Time I Listened Well to Someone."

Can you remember a time when you really paid attention to someone and listened carefully to what he or she said. This means that you didn't interrupt with your own ideas or daydream about your own plans, but really concentrated and tried to understand what the other person was attempting to get across. Maybe you've listened to a friend like that, or a younger brother or sister, or a teacher or coach. Think about it for a few moments and, if you wish, tell us about, "A Time I Listened Well to Someone."

Discussion Questions:

1. *What kinds of things make listening difficult?*
2. *Why is it important to listen to others?*
3. *What could you do to improve your listening?*
4. *How do you feel when someone really listens to you?*

One of the Nicest Things a Friend Ever Did for Me
A Sharing Circle

Objectives:

The students will:
— express the need to belong.
— describe how friends contribute to each other's enjoyment and wellbeing.

Introduce the Topic:

Today we're going to talk about the special moments that we have shared with our friends. Our topic is, "One of the Nicest Things a Friend Ever Did for Me. "

Think of something that a friend did for you that you really appreciated. Perhaps it was totally spontaneous, like suddenly saying, "you're terrific. " Or maybe it was carefully planned, like a surprise party or a special gift. Or your friend may simply have listened to you when you needed to talk. Some of the most meaningful moments between friends are simple and involve no money and almost no effort at all. Think about it for a few moments. The topic is, "One of the Nicest Things a Friend Ever Did for Me.

Discussion Questions:

1. *What similarities or differences did you notice in the things we shared?*

2. *How can you show a friend that you appreciate what he or she has done for you?*

3. *How do you feel about asking a friend for help when you need it?*

Something I Never Do When
I Want to Make Friends
A Sharing Circle

Objectives:

The students will:
— express the need to belong.
— identify behaviors that can act as deterrents to friendship.

Introduce the Topic:

What things do you purposely avoid doing if you like someone? Maybe you're careful not to be bossy or dominate conversations. Maybe you try not to be nosey, or make negative comments about what the person says or wears. Perhaps you've learned from experience that people are turned off *by constant complaining or clowning around. Think about it for a few moments. The topic is, "Something I Never Do When I Want to Make Friends. "*

Discussion Questions:

1. *Why do you avoid the behavior you mentioned?*

2. *Why is it important to know how to make friends?*

3. *What are the benefits and risks of telling others about the things they do that turn us off?*

4. *What can you do if you have trouble making friends and aren't sure why?*

INCLUSION AND INTERDEPENDENCE

Appreciating and valuing similarities and differences is not only important to maintaining good relationships, it is critical to bringing individuals to a level of full participation in any venture. One of the oldest sources of conflict between individuals and groups is lack of understanding between people who are different with respect to such things as race, religion, appearance, lifestyle, cultural values, and physical or mental disabilities. To build understanding, individuals must recognize the role and Power of expectations, and realize that imposing expectations on others without their participation leads to the breakdown of relationships. They must also recognize the consequences of exclusion, and experience the power and joy of collaboration.

Activities in this unit help students examine the limitations and personal pain that they and others have experienced as a direct result exclusion. Participants are encouraged to recognize various forms of exclusion in the social behaviors of themselves and their peers, and to consider the benefits of opening their groups to wider participation. Simulations, experiments, and games help young people to experience inclusion and interdependence, and to regard these conditions as the mortar of teams and support groups sources of strength and power, enabling and supporting the richness of diversity.

Search for the One Person Team
Group Discussion and Experience Sheet

Objectives:

The students will:
— state that successful teams are characterized by diversity.
— identify specific differences that have contributed to a successful group endeavor.
— distinguish between individual and group identity.
— distinguish between interdependence and dependence.

Materials:

one copy of the experience sheet "Search for the One Person Team" for each student

Directions:

Introduce the experience sheet by making the point that rarely is a successful endeavor accomplished by one person acting alone. Even when just one person appears to have carried out a project singlehandedly, there are always other people in the background without whose cooperation and collaboration the finished product would not have been achieved.

Announce to the students that you want each of them to identify a group that is diverse and interdependent, and identify the different skills and talents that make the group successful. Explain that the students may choose any type of group they wish: a band, singing group, athletic team, club, business, etc. The group may be one to which they belong, or it may be a group they have observed in action or read about. A solo performer who works with a backup team or a support crew may also be considered a group.

Pass out the experience sheet, "Search for the One Person Team," and announce that they will have about 15 minutes to complete the sheet.

When the students have completed their experience sheets, ask volunteers to tell the class about the diverse makeup of the group they selected. After those students who wish to have shared, make the following points:

- No one can succeed in complete isolation.
- We all have gifts to contribute and those gifts are needed somewhere.
- Generally speaking, teams accomplish more than individuals accomplish.
- When we choose to be *interdependent* with others, we are not becoming a *dependent* person, we are joining our resources with the resources of others in a common effort.

Conclude the activity by facilitating further discussion.

Discussion Questions:

1. *What is the difference between interdependence and dependence?*

2. *What kinds of diversity are essential for groups to be successful?*

3. *When you think about the group or team you selected, do you appraise the group by considering individual members or by considering the group as a whole? Why do you think that is?*

4. *Can you think of an individual who succeeded at something without interdepending with others?*

Search for the One-Person Team
Experience Sheet

When people come together, they bring all of their unique personalities, viewpoints, talents, and skills. When they apply these differences to achieving a common goal, wonderful things often happen. Take a moment to think of some groups and teams with which you are familiar. Pick a group or team that you think is successful because each member brings something unique and vital to the process. Then complete the following:

Group Name:

_____

What the group does:

_____

_____

What talents and/or skills does each member of the group have?

_____

_____

_____

_____

_____

What diverse physical characteristics can you identify among this group's members?

_____

_____

_____

_____

Can you name the members of this group? List as many names as you can remember:

_____

_____

_____

_____

_____

What makes this group stand out?

_____

_____

_____

_____

_____

Getting In at Our School
Interviews, Investigations, and Oral Reports

Objectives:

The students will:
— identify on- and off-campus organizations and extracurricular activities.
— demonstrate strategies for building positive peer support systems.
— explain how the needs of students with disabilities can be met within organizations.

Materials:

5-inch by 8-inch file cards

Directions:

Begin this activity by talking with the students about the importance of peer support. Ask them if they are aware of the fact that each time they make a friend, join an organization, help another student, or participate in a group activity, they are building a peer support group network of people they can turn to for:

- companionship and sharing
- help with projects and problems
- backing in reaching goals or making changes
- cooperation when a group effort is required
- protection if they're threatened or coerced
- creativity when new ideas are called for

Suggest that one of the best ways to strengthen and enlarge one's peer support group is to become involved in extracurricular activities and on- and off-campus organizations. Point out that joining lots of organizations is not necessarily the objective that simply becoming informed about an organization and making contact with one or two of its leaders can bring the entire organization within one's own network of resources.

Choose two or three students to develop a list of on-campus organizations and a second group to develop a list of off-campus organizations (including volunteer opportunities) suitable for teens. Meet briefly with the groups and brainstorm methods that they can use to conduct their research. Give them about 1 week to complete the assignment.

Pass around the lists of organizations and ask every student in class to sign up to do an indepth investigation of one of them. Encourage the students to work in groups of two or three. Suggest that the students attend a meeting and/or talk to a leader of the organization and provide the following information on a 5 X 8 index card:

1. Name of the organization
2. Affiliated inside or outside of school
3. Purpose of the organization
4. Types of activities and location and frequency of meetings
5. Qualifications to join
6. Procedure to join
7. What steps are taken to accommodate a wide range of students?
8. Name of contact person or sponsor and room/phone number
9. Time and place of next meeting

Ask two or three students (or groups of students) a day to report their findings to the class. Post the index cards on a bulletin board for a week or two. Then organize them in a file box. Lead a followup discussion.

Discussion Questions:

1. *What organizations sound particularly interesting to you? Why?*

2. *How are organizations formed?*

3. *If you wanted to start an organization for students, how could you begin the process?*

4. *How do organizations benefit by including all interested students?*

Extension:

Ask the class to choose three organizations that it would like to learn more about and invite a leader from each one to visit the class and make a brief (10 to 15minute presentation.

How It Feels To Be Left Out
Creative Writing and Discussion

Objectives:

The students will:
— describe in writing how a person with a disability might feel in response to being excluded.
— describe behavioral choices available in response to rejection/exclusion.

Materials:

writing materials

Directions:

Explain to the students that you would like them to write about the topic, "How It Feels to Be Left Out." Emphasize that they will need to use their imaginations, because they are going to write from the viewpoint of a person with a disability.

In your own words, explain to the students: *Imagine a situation in which a person with a disability might be excluded. Think about how you feel when you are left out of a group or activity that you really want to participate in. How might the situation and/or the feelings be the same or different for someone with a disability? If the feelings would be about the same, what would they be? If the feelings would be different, how would they be different, and what would they be like? You might begin your story when the person is just starting to think about joining the group or activity. Describe what happens that leads to the rejection, and concentrate on the expression of feelings throughout.*

Ask the students to indicate at the end of their papers whether or not they would be willing to read their story to the class. Collect the papers and evaluate them in your usual manner, then return them to the students. At a subsequent class meeting, ask volunteers to read their stories to the class. Facilitate a discussion after each reading, basing your questions on issues presented in the story. Conclude the activity with a discussion.

Discussion Questions:

1. *How are the feelings of people with and without disabilities the same in response to rejection? How are they different?*

2. *What inaccuracies did you discover in your own perceptions of people who have disabilities?*

3. *What good does it do to try to understand each other's feelings?*

4. *What new ideas did you get about rejecting others? ... about handling rejection? ... about the concept of full inclusion?*

The Reason for Cliques
Brainstorming, Discussion, and Experience Sheet

Objectives:

The students will:
— identify ways to make new friends.
— define the term *clique* and describe the effects of cliques.
— state how they can avoid making other people feel left out.

Materials:

the experience sheet, "What Would You Do?" for each student; whiteboard or chart paper

Directions:

Have the students form two teams. Give the teams 10 to 15 minutes to brainstorm a list describing as many ways as they can think of to make new friends. At the end of the allotted time, reconvene the class and ask the groups to share their lists. Possible ideas include:

- Sit beside someone different in the cafeteria and say hello.
- Offer to show someone new around the school.
- Join a school organization.
- Offer to help someone carry a heavy load.
- Team up with someone you don't know very well to work on a class project.
- Run an ad in the school paper asking for a companion for particular activities, like hiking or bicycling.
- Ask someone you know to introduce you to new people.
- Go to the gym or track after school and say hello to the kids who are practicing.

Write the word *clique* on the board and ask the students to help you define it. One possible definition might be:

An in-group or gang of popular kids that defines itself
as much by who is excluded as by who is included

Discuss how a clique's policy of exclusion causes members to have difficulty making new friends, and can completely frustrate the efforts of someone who is not in the clique to become good friends with someone who is. Stress that the reason many kids want to be a part of a clique is that they want to be liked by "important" people and feel important themselves.

Ask the students to turn to the experience sheet, "What Would You Do?" Allow the students about 10 minutes to complete the sheet. Then ask them to rejoin their teams and (voluntarily) share their answers to the questions.

Encourage the students to commit to making one new friend before the next session or to including one new person in their existing group of friends. Stipulate that before they can claim to have completed this assignment, the students must do something tangible with the new friend, such as sit together at an assembly, eat lunch together, go jogging or bicycling together, visit each other's home, see a movie together, or play video games after school. Ask the students to pay particular attention to the "clique phenomenon" and avoid doing anything that causes another person to feel left out. Conclude the activity with a discussion.

Discussion Questions:

1. *In what ways do you think cliques are good?*

2. *In what ways do you think cliques are harmful?*

3. *Have you ever wanted to belong to a clique? If so, why was it important?*

4. *What would happen if there were no cliques at this school?*

5. *What kinds of cliques do adults have?*

What Would You Do?
Experience Sheet

Is it worth it to be in? What have you done to be included in a group? **I have...**
YES or NO

_____ _____ risked losing friends.

_____ _____ hurt people who thought they were my friends by making them feel left out.

_____ _____ done something I thought was not right.

_____ _____ done something I knew was against the law.

_____ _____ drunk alcohol or used drugs.

_____ _____ done something that might have harmed me physically.

_____ _____ done something that cost me a lot of money.

_____ _____ done something that interfered with my school work.

_____ _____ done something my parents would have objected to if they had known.

_____ _____ done whatever was necessary, as long as it didn't harm anyone else.

_____ _____ done something that was against my religion.

_____ _____ done whatever was necessary.

Can you remember a time when you were pressured to exclude someone from an activity?

How did you feel? _____

_____

_____

_____

What did you do? _____

_____

_____

_____

_____

_____

_____

_____

If this ever happens again, what do you think you will do?

_____

_____

_____

_____

Are We The Same or Different?
Presentation and Group Discussion

Objectives:

The students will:
— name specific ways in which people are different and the same.
— demonstrate that individual perception determines whether a characteristic is seen as a difference or a commonality.
— recognize commonalties as vital to achieving understanding and harmony.
— describe differences as vital to achieving success.

Materials:

whiteboard or chart paper

Directions:

Draw a horizontal line on the board, dividing a section of the board approximately in half. At the top of the board, write the heading, "Different." Begin the activity by asking the students to name all of the ways that human beings differ from one another. Write their suggestions below the heading. You will probably list such items as personality, preferences, skills, intelligence, traditions, culture, race, gender, abilities, physical appearance, socioeconomic status, etc. Keep going until the space above the line is crowded with items.

Write the heading, "Same," at the top of the lower section of board, just below the line. Ask the students to name all of the ways in which humans are exactly the same. Suggestions will come more slowly this time. Be patient and see if someone comes up with the idea that all the items written above the line also represent ways in which people are exactly alike. (The idea is that all people possess personalities, skills, intelligence, etc., even though these attributes differ qualitatively from one person to another. In fact, this can be said for every item written above the line. All of these things not only make people different, they also make them the same.) If one of the students makes this observation, proceed from there. If no one discovers the concept, explain that you can add greatly to the list, and begin underlining items above the line, saying something like, "We all have different personalities, but we all have a personality, etc." Make the point that people are as much alike as they are different.

Explain that whether we see these items as differences or commonalties depends on our perception. When we focus only on the ways we differ, we tend to grow apart, but when we focus on commonalties, we tend to come together. This coming together creates strength in diversity. It can be thought of, too, as *unity through diversity* or *common ground*

Tell the students that ALL successful teams are built on diversity. Using the example of personalities, demonstrate how everyone on a team has an individual personality, and that together those personalities make up the team personality. Members have different talents, skills, and knowledge to bring to a team. These differences are what make teams strong. Without diversity, a team cannot have much strength.

When individuals believe that their differences make them right or better (and make others wrong or worse) conflicts occur. The need to see our differences as "right" or "wrong" destroys our ability to work together effectively.

Discussion Questions:

1. *What are some ways in which all people benefit from individual differences?*

2. *How can differences among group members contribute to their efforts when working on a joint endeavor?*

3. *How does the need to be "right" interfere with efforts to build on diversity?*

4. *How can understanding the commonalities of all people help you in your relationships now? ...in your future?*

Counting on Each Other
Experience Sheet and Discussion

Objectives:

The students will:
— identify specific ways in which people "count on" one another.
— name specific ways in which they count on individual classmates.
— explain why it is important for people to rely on one another.
— define trust and explain how it develops.

Materials:

one copy of the experience sheet, "Count on Me" for each student; whiteboard and marker

Directions:

Ask the students to help you brainstorm some of the many different ways people count on one another in the classroom and elsewhere. List their ideas on the board or chart paper. To facilitate, ask such questions as, "What do we count on each other for?""What do you count on me for?" "What do you count on your parents for?" "What do you count on your neighbors for?" "What do you count on your best friend for?" Write their ideas on the board. Include such items as:

I count on _____ to help me solve problems.
    … spend leisure time with me.
    … make me laugh.
    … listen when I talk.
    … keep a confidence.
    … help with responsibilities at home.
    … help with school assignments.
    … tell the truth.
    … understand me.
    … answer my questions.
    … love me.
    … be fair in games and sports.
    … protect me.
    … do a good job.
    … be on time.
    … keep a promise.

Ask the students to turn to the experience sheet. Announce that you want the students to think about the unique qualities, talents, and abilities of each person in the class and write down one way in which they count on that person. Tell them to use the list on the board for ideas. If the group or class is very large, have the students complete this assigmnent in smaller groups. Existing work groups would be ideal.

When the students have finished, call on individual students to read what they have written. Repeat this process until all students have been identified with what others count on them for. Conclude with a class discussion.

Discussion Questions:

1. *How do you feel knowing that you can count on so many people?*

2. *How do we learn to rely on other people?*

3. *How do you let others know they can count on you?*

4. *How does knowing you can count on someone build trust?*

5. *Why is trust important in any endeavor where people are working together?*

Count on Me
Experience Sheet

Take a few minutes to think about your classmates or the members of your work group. Write down each person's name. Then, think about that person's unique qualities, talents, and abilities. How does that person contribute to the group? What is one way in which you count on that person?

I can count on _____ to _____ .

I can count on _____ to _____ .

I can count on _____ to _____ .

I can count on _____ to _____ .

I can count on _____ to _____ .

I can count on _____ to _____ .

I can count on _____ to _____ .

I can count on _____ to _____ .

I can count on _____ to _____ .

I can count on _____ to _____ .

I can count on _____ to _____ .

I can count on _____ to _____ .

I can count on _____ to _____ .

I can count on _____ to _____ .

I can count on _____ to _____ .

I can count on _____ to _____ .

I can count on _____ to _____ .

I can count on _____ to _____ .

I can count on _____ to _____ .

I can count on _____ to _____ .

My classmates can count on me to:

1. _____

2. _____

3. _____

4. _____

5. _____

I Wanted to Be Part of a Group, But Was Left Out
A Sharing Circle

Objectives:

The students will:
— understand and express the need to belong.
— describe an incident in which they were excluded.
— explain how the need to belong can influence individual behavior.

Introduce the Topic:

One of the most important things to most young people is fitting in and belonging to a group. Although this need continues into adulthood, it is particularly strong during adolescence because this is the time when the skills of group membership are learned. It is one of the main "developmental tasks" of this period of life. Today, we're going to look at what happens when we are refused membership in a group for some reason. We're going to talk about the feelings we experience when we are excluded. Our topic is, "I Wanted to Be Part of a Group, But Was Left Out. "

Think back to a time when you really wanted to do something with a group of friends or an organization, but you weren't invited. How did you feel? What did you do? Maybe you tried out for a part in a play or a musical group and didn't make it. How long did it take you to get over it? Have you ever heard some friends talking about something fun they did over the weekend and felt hurt because you weren't asked to join them? Have you ever tried to join in a conversation and been completely ignored? Have you ever felt that you were excluded because you were poorer than the other members of the group, or of a different race, or had a disability? Think about it for a few moments. If you decide to share, describe the situation and tell us how you handled your feelings. Our topic is, "I Wanted to Be Part of a Group, But Was Left Out.

Discussion Questions:

1. *What did you feel like doing when you were left out? What did you do?*

2. *How long did it take you to get over your hurt feelings?*

3. *If a group rejects you because you refuse to conform to its code of behavior, what's the best thing to do?*

4. *What advice would you give a friend who seemed willing to do almost anything to fit in with a group?*

5. *How do attitudes of exclusion hurt us?*

A Time I Worked in a Successful Group
A Sharing Circle

Objectives:

The students will:
— describe characteristics of a successful group.
— describe their contributions to the success of a group.
— state that a successful group needs the diverse abilities of all its members.

Introduce the Topic:

All of us have belonged to a group that has had some form of success. Successful groups have certain characteristics in common. One of these characteristics is interdependence. Interdependence exists when the strength of the group is built on the contributions of its members and the members derive benefits from being part of the group. Today, we are going to look at an experience of our own to explore the characteristics of interdependence. In the process, we're going to discover some other characteristics of successful groups. Our topic is, "A Time I Worked in a Successful Group. "

Think of one time when you were a part of a group that achieved something significant. The group might have been a team, or a work group with a particular task to complete. Maybe it was a family group, or a social or religious group. It might even have been a bunch of friends working together. Whatever the group, focus on its achievements. What made the group successful? What were some of the characteristics of the group that caused it to function so well? How did you feel when you were part of this group. Take a moment to think about all of these things. The topic is, "A Time I Worked in a Successful Group.

Discussion Questions:

1. *How did members of the group feel toward one another?*

2. *What were some of the contributions that different people made to the success of the groups we discussed?*

3. *In what ways can groups outperform individuals?*

4. *Under what circumstances can individuals accomplish more alone?*

5. *What are some characteristics besides interdependence that make groups successful?*

COMMUNICATION AND CONVERSATIONAL SKILLS

Effective communication is critical to success and leadership in all areas. While it seems only natural that humans should equitably exchange their thoughts and feelings, many have not acquired the skills necessary to communicate with the understanding and empathy needed to build and bend relationships. One of the major reasons we experience problems in communication is that we forget that individual experiences are never identical. Yet when we develop a closer understanding of what others experience, we find more agreement than disagreement. In this unit students have an opportunity to examine their successes and shortcomings in communication, identify roadblocks to effective communication and develop skills for listening and expressing themselves. Skills that are necessary in all successful life endeavors.

Communication Stoppers
Role-Play and Discussion

Objectives:

The students will:
— demonstrate common ways of responding to another person that may block communication.
— describe how different ways of responding may affect a speaker.
— discuss what constitutes effective and ineffective communication

Materials:

a copy of the "Six Communication Stoppers" and "Communications Stoppers Role Plays"experience sheets for each student

Directions:

Write the following list on the board or chart paper for the students to see when they enter class:

- Interrupting
- Advising
- Dominating
- Over Questioning
- Contradicting
- Criticizing/Putting-downs

Begin the activity by asking the students to think of a heading or title for the list on the board. Write their suggestions down and discuss each one briefly. Add the suggested title, "Communication Stoppers." Pass out the experience sheet "Six Communication Stoppers" to each student. Discuss the communication stoppers further by asking the students if they can imagine how these behaviors might have the effect of hampering communication—or stopping it altogether.

Ask the students to role-play each behavior to see what kind of effect it does have on communication. Invite volunteers to form teams of two. Assign a communication stopper to each team and pass out the "Communication Stoppers Role Play" sheet to the teams. Ask the teams to briefly discuss how they can demonstrate their communication stopper to the rest of the class using the role play suggestions on their sheet.

Encourage the students to use appropriate gestures, volume, and tone to make their role play as convincing as possible. Tell them to continue demonstrating their particular communication stopper until the student trying to share gives up talking, or the point has been sufficiently made.

After each demonstration, lead a brief discussion about the effects of that communication stopper (see Discussion Questions). Below are points to make about each communication stopper as the discussions ensue.

Interrupting

Point out how frustrating it is to be interrupted, and how futile it is to continue a conversation when interruptions occur over and over. Interrupting is probably the most frequent way in which communication is stopped.

Advising

By giving unsolicited advice, a person immediately assumes a position of superiority. Advice-giving says, "I know better than you do." Advice may also cause the speaker to feel powerless to control his or her own life.

Dominating

We all know how frustrating and annoying it is to be in a conversation with someone who always has something better and more interesting to say than we do. In addition, when one person dominates a conversation, others are forced to use another communication stopper, interrupting, just to get a word in.

Over Questioning

Asking too many questions tends to put the speaker on the defensive by asking him or her to justify or explain every statement. More importantly, questions may lead the speaker away from what she or he originally wanted to say. The questioner thus controls the conversation and its direction.

Contradicting

Contradictions and accusations put the speaker on the spot, and make it necessary for her or him to take a defensive position. They also say to the speaker, "You are wrong." or "You are bad."

Criticizing/Putting-down

Criticism diminishes the speaker. Few of us want to continue a conversation in which we are being diminished. Put-downs are frequently veiled in humor, but may nonetheless be hurtful and damaging to a relationship and can certainly end a conversation.

In addition to making the points above use the following discussion questions after each demonstration to get the students to focus on the effects of each communication stopper.

Discussion Questions:

1. *How did you (the speaker) feel?*

2. *What effect does this type of response have on the speaker? ...on the conversation? ...on the relationship?*

3. *Has this ever happened to you? What did you say and/or do?*

4. *Under what circumstances would it be okay to respond like this?*

Six Communication Stoppers
Experience Sheet

Have you ever paid attention to how you communicate with others? Think about what it's like to have a conversation with someone who won't let you finish a sentence. Or, how about trying to talk about a problem you're having with someone who has an answer for everything. Bad communication habits tend to cut conversations short. Here are six communication stoppers to be aware of and to try to avoid in your conversations with others:

Interrupting
Interruptions are the most common cause of stalled communication. It's frustrating to be interrupted in the middle of a sentence, and when interruptions happen over and over again, talking begins to feel like a waste of time.

Dominating
We all know how frustrating and annoying it is to be in a conversation with someone who think they always have something better and more interesting to say than we do. In addition, when you dominate a conversation, others are forced to use another communication stopper, *interrupting*, just to get a word in.

Advising
Few people enjoy getting unasked-for advice. Statements that begin with, "Well, if I were you...," or "If you ask me...," are like red flags. Advice-giving says, "I'm superior. I know better than you do." Advice can also cause a person to feel powerless— as though she can't make a good decision on her own.

Over Questioning
Asking a lot of questions ("Why did you go there?" "Who did you see?" "What did he do?") tends to put the speaker on the defensive by requiring her to explain every statement. More importantly, your questions may lead the speaker *away from* what she originally wanted to say. If you ask too many questions, you are controlling, not sharing, the conversation.

Contradicting

There's nothing more frustrating than trying to talk with someone who challenges everything you say, insists that your ideas are wrong, or states that what happened was your fault. Contradictions and accusations put the speaker on the spot, and make the speaker defensive.

Criticizing/Putting-down

Don't make sarcastic or negative remarks in response to the things someone says. Criticism whittles away at self-esteem. Hardly anyone wants to continue a conversation that's making him feel bad or small. Even put-downs that sound funny can still be hurtful. In the long run, they damage friendships.

Communication Stoppers Role Plays
Experience Sheet

Interrupting: Butt in time and again as the speaker talks, with statements about yourself and things that have happened to you. For example, if the student says, "I have a friend named Sue, and...," interrupt with, "Oh, I know her—well, a little. We met the other day when...etc., etc."

Advising: Give lots of unasked-for advice. Use statements like, "Well, if I were you...," "I think you should...," and "Have you tried..." If the speaker says, "I have a friend named Sue, and...," respond with, "Sue has a lot of problems. Take my advice and steer clear or her." or "Be careful what you tell Sue. She can't keep a secret for three minutes." Etc.

Dominating: Take over the conversation. If the student says, "I have a friend named Sue, and...," jump in with, "I know Sue's brother. He is..., and not only that, he..., and so..., because..., blah, blah, blah, etc., etc., ad nauseam.

Over-Questioning: Ask question after question in a demanding tone. If the student says, "I have a friend named Sue, and...," ask, "Why do you hang out with her?" As soon as the student begins to answer, ask, "How long have you known her?" "Is her hair naturally blonde?" And so on.

Contradicting: Contradict what the student says and accuse him or her of being wrong. For example, if the student says, "I have a friend named Sue, and...," say, "She's not really your friend. You know her because she's Anna's friend." If the student says, "Sue and I have a lot in common." say, "You're dreaming. Name one thing!"

Criticizing/Putting-down: Make sarcastic, negative remarks in response to everything the student says. If the student says, "I have a friend named Sue, and...," say, "You jerk, what are you hanging out with her for." If the student says, "Because I like her..." respond, "You never did have good sense."

Words Are Only Part of It
Dramatizations and Discussion

Objectives:

The students will

— demonstrate that communication involves much more than the simple transmission of words and ideas.

— discuss how feelings are conveyed in communication.

Materials:

a copy of the "Body Talk" experience sheet for each student

Directions:

Prior to class, write the following words on the board:

delight	confusion	surprise	worry	hate
sadness	love	irritation	anger	fear

Begin the activity by briefly reviewing the list of words with the students. Point out that these are just some of the many emotions people feel. Point out that communication involves much more than the simple use of words. Emotions get into the act in a number of ways.

Illustrate the point by silently selecting one of the emotions listed on the board and asking the class to guess which one it is while you repeat a tongue twister. Say the tongue twister and, with your tone, inflection, facial expression, posture, and movements, simultaneously convey the emotion you selected. After the laughter subsides, allow the students to guess which emotion you were trying to convey. Then ask them how they knew. List the clues they mention on the board.

Repeat the tongue twister once or twice, conveying other emotions from the list. Discuss with the class the specific tones, inflection, facial expressions, body postures, and movements you used to express each feeling.

Invite the students to demonstrate other emotions. Have volunteers come to the front of the class and repeat the process. Introduce a new tongue twister from time to time. After each demonstration, ask the class to examine the manner in which the emotion was communicated. Ask questions such as:

1. *Can you describe the tone and inflection?*
2. *What did his face do?*
3. *What was her posture like?*
4. *How did she move her body?*

Tongue Twisters

- Rubber baby-buggy bumpers
- She sells sea shells down by the sea shore.
- Peter Piper picked a peck of pickled peppers.
- How much wood would a woodchuck chuck if a woodchuck could chuck wood?
- Big black bugs bleed blood.

After some or all of the emotions listed have been demonstrated, vary the activity. Restrict what the performers can do. First, ask them not to move their bodies in any way, using words, tone, and inflection only. Second, ask them to convey the emotion completely nonverbally, depending only on facial expressions, posture, and body language.

Pass out the "Body Talk" experience sheet to the students. Give them a few minutes to fill it out. Lead a follow-up discussion.

Discussion Questions:

1. *How do people communicate without words?*

2. *Why do you think tongue twisters were used in our dramatizations, instead of important ideas?*

3. *How can you hide your feelings when you are communicating with someone? What effect does that have on communication?*

4. *How can being aware of your body language help when you're trying to communicate important information?*

5. *What did you learn from this activity? ...from the experience sheet?*

Body Talk
Experience Sheet

You communicate with your body all the time. As you react emotionally to events in your life, your body takes on different postures and positions.

Think of a time recently when you experienced the following emotions. What did you do with your body? How do you think your body looked to others? Describe your body language below:

Embarrassment: _____
_____
_____
_____

Nervousness: _____
_____
_____
_____

Excitement: _____
_____
_____
_____

Boredom: _____
_____
_____
_____

Words and Symbols
Communication Experiments and Discussion

Objectives:

The students will:
— participate in a conversation in which everyone has limited physical senses.
— participate in a conversation in which one person uses graphic symbols to communicate.
— describe how vision, observation, and graphic decoding contribute to communication.

Materials:

scarves, large handkerchiefs, or strips of opaque fabric to use as blindfolds; a list of conversation topics written on the board; the experience sheet, "Communicating With Graphics," for each student.

Directions:

Announce that the students are going to participate in two experiments in which communication will take place with limited physical senses. In the first, vision and the ability to observe will be lost. In the second, one partner will communicate with no speech and only limited movement.

Have the students sit together in groups of four. Allow the groups about 1 minute to agree on a conversation topic (from the list on the board). Then distribute the blindfolds and allow another minute or so for the students to blindfold themselves or each other.

Have the groups discuss their topic for 10 to 15 minutes. Then ask them to remove their blindfolds and, remaining in their small groups, share their reactions to the experience.

Next, have the groups of four divide into two pairs. Pass out the experience sheet, "Communicating With Graphics," to the students. Briefly review the symbols and discuss their meanings with the students. Explain that the pairs are going to have two more short conversations, again using topics from the board. In each conversation, one partner will communicate by pointing one elbow to the graphic symbols on the page or to other things within his or her immediate environment. This partner has limited movement ability and may neither speak nor move, other than to turn his/her head and move one arm in order to point with the elbow of that arm. The other partner must attempt to decode the graphic symbols, translate the decoded communication into words to make sure he/she is understanding, and then respond in words.

Give the partners a moment to choose a topic from the board and decide who will be first to use the graphic mode of communication. Then allow at least 5 minutes for the first conversation. Call time and have the partners switch roles, choose another topic, and have the second conversation for at least 5 minutes. Lead a follow-up class discussion.

Discussion Questions:

1. *What was it like to have a conversation with everyone blindfolded?*

2. *What did you notice about your own listening during this experiment? What did you notice about your speaking?*

3. *What did being sightless demonstrate to you about the role of vision in communication?*

4. *How did you feel while using only the graphic mode of communication?*

5. *What was it like to converse in words with someone who talked in symbols?*

6. *What did you learn about communication from this experiment?*

7. *What did you learn from either of these experiments about communicating with people who have disabilities?*

Suggested Conversation Topics

"Highlights of My Daily Routine"
"My Favorite Saturday (or Sunday) Afternoon"
"Something I Want to Accomplish"
"A Way I Earn Money"
"How I Help Out at Home"
"My Favorite Vacation"
"If I Could Go Anywhere, I'd..."
"A Problem I'm Trying to Solve"
"What I Would Do If I Had A Million Dollars"
"My Plans for College Or A Career"

Communicating with Graphics
Experience Sheet

Graphic mode communication involves the use of symbols to represent actual objects. There are many kinds of graphic symbols. The most commonly used include line drawings, photographs, and product logos.

Graphic mode communication is a form of **alternative communication**. People who use alternative forms of communication are unable to communicate using spoken language or writing, and rely exclusively on signs, gestures, or graphic symbols to communicate. Other people have a limited ability to speak or write and use graphic symbols to help them communicate better. This is called **augmentative communication**. Conditions that result in a need for an alternative or augmentative system include *cerebral palsy, mental retardation, spinal cord injury, multiple sclerosis, muscular dystrophy, Parkinson's disease,* and *ALS*. Sometimes the need for an alternative or augmentative system is temporary, such as when a person loses her speech temporarily due to an accident or surgery.

Choose a partner. By pointing to the symbols on these pages (and to real objects around you in the room), see if you can carry on a short conversation with your partner. Your partner may speak, but you may not.

family	dog	cat	bird
horse	bicycle	car	bus
clothes	hat, cap	jacket	flower

tree	telephone	TV	clock, time
present	music	travel, bag	money
camera	movie	stairs	party
peach	pie	pear	potato
tomato	sandwich	salad	spaghetti
pizza	taco	soda	water

dance	cook	eat	drive
fight	walk	run	give
build	laugh	sing	cry
think	buy, pay	love	shop
cut	building	house	city
mountains	camp	beach	school

A Time When I Accepted Someone Else's Feelings
A Sharing Circle

Objectives:

The students will:
— describe the need all people have to be accepted.
— identify positive and negative feelings that they have experienced.
— describe specific examples of their own pro-social behavior.

Introduce the Topic:

Say to the students: *It means a lot to all of us to have our feelings accepted. When someone accepts your feelings, it's the same as accepting you. In this session, we are going to turn this idea around and talk about how it feels to be the <u>giver</u> of acceptance. The topic is "A Time When I Accepted Someone Else's Feelings."*

Can you remember a time when you gave attention to someone else and accepted his or her feelings? Keep in mind that accepting feelings may mean accepting feelings that are different from you own, without getting angry or judging the other person. Think of a time when you did this, and tell us about it. The topic is, "A Time When I Accepted Someone Else's Feelings."

Discussion Questions:

1. *When is it easy to accept someone else's feelings? When is it hard?*

2. *Have you ever been unable to accept someone's feelings and not known why? What was going on inside you at that time?*

3. *How do you show a person that you accept his or her feelings?*

4. *How did the person whose feelings you accepted seem to feel about you?*

A Way I Let Others Know I'm Interested In What They Say
A Sharing Circle

Objective:

The students will:
— describe specific ways they behave when listening to others that convey their interest in what is being discussed.

Introduce the Topic:

Say to the students: *Our topic for this session is, "A Way I Let Others Know I'm Interested in What They Say." One way we can let another person know that we are listening and interested in what they have to say is by what we say in response. There are many other things we can do, too. Some of these involve our posture, the way we make eye contact, or whether or how frequently we interrupt them. Think of some of the ways you show other people that you are interested in what they are saying. Also think about how you feel when others listen to you with interest. Select one of the ways you show interest and tell us about it, if you'd like. Our topic is, "A Way I Let Others Know I'm Interested in What They Say."*

Discussion Questions:

1. *How do you think people feel knowing that you are really interested in what they have to say?*

2. *How do you feel knowing that others are interested in what you have to say?*

3. *What things can a person do to become a more effective listener or communicator?*

A Time When I Really Felt Heard
A Sharing Circle

Objectives:

The students will:
— describe the importance of listening in the communication process.
— describe feelings generated by being recognized and heard.

Introduce the Topic:

Say to the students: *Today our topic is, "A Time I Really Felt Heard." We know that attention is a universal need. Sometimes we do not get it for one reason or another, but when we do our feelings are generally positive.*

Think of a time when you really needed to be heard and someone listened to you. Perhaps you had some kind of a problem that you wanted to talk out, or maybe you had an experience that you wanted to tell someone about. Who listened to you? How did you feel after you had expressed yourself? Think about it for a few moments. The topic is, "A Time When I Really Felt Heard."

Discussion Questions:

1. *How are people generally affected when their feelings are not accepted?*

2. *Do people keep their feelings to themselves because they think they won't be accepted?*

3. *When people risk saying how they feel, do others respect them for it? Do you? Why or why not?*

4. *How did you feel about the person who listened to you?*

5. *How did you feel about yourself?*

6. *What happens to communication when people don't listen well?*

What I Think Good Communication Is
A Sharing Circle

Objectives:

The students will:
— identify specific components of effective communication.
— state specific reasons why good communication is important.

Introduce the Topic:

Today's topic for discussion is, "What I Think Good Communication Is". Communication is an exchange of thoughts, feelings, opinions, or information between two or more people. Today we're going to focus on the ingredients of good communication. There are no right or wrong answers; whatever you contribute will help us develop a better understanding of what's involved. If you like, try thinking about a person with whom you've had particular success communicating and attempt to isolate some of the things that happen during your interactions with that person. Take a few minutes, and then we'll begin sharing on our topic, "What I Think Good Communication Is."

Discussion Questions:

1. *What quality or ingredient of good communication was mentioned most often during our sharing?*

2. *Why is it important to practice good communication?*

3. *How can understanding how to communicate effectively help you in college? ...in your career?*

SETTING AND ATTAINING GOALS

Little is accomplished without first being the subject of a well articulated goal. The magic in goal setting is that it allows resources to come together to accomplish just about anything, and marshalling resources is a prime task of successful endeavors. We often think of goals in a global context, but all successful people set goals in their personal lives. Goals are stepping stones to well defined futures. They provide a sense of direction and permit decisions that advance goal attainment.

In this unit, activities enable students to clarify their expectations, values, likes, dislikes, and dreams in preparation for setting clear, realistic goals. Participants learn the importance of having an overriding vision and of aligning and attuning goals to support their vision. A goal setting process is presented in detail and participants are asked to set specific, measurable goals in various areas. They learn to develop plans for accomplishing their goals, and they support those goals through the techniques of visualization and affirmation. Finally, participants consider the value of rewarding themselves at each major milestone they reach.

The Power of Expectations
Discussion and Sharing Circles

Objectives:

The students will:
— discuss the differences between their self expectations and the expectations they have of others.
— differentiate reasonable and unreasonable expectations.
— describe how expectations shape behavior.

Materials:

whiteboard or chart paper

Directions:

Relate to the students the story of *My Fair Lady* as described in the following synopsis:

At one time, the idea that people could change themselves for the better was thought impossible. For example, if you were born poor, the expectation was that you would remain poor for the rest of your life. You could not improve or change. A writer and philosopher who believed that people could be transformed, could change and become different was George Bernard Shaw. He said, "People are always blaming their circumstances for what they are. I don't believe in circumstances. The people who get on in this world are the people who get up and look for the circumstances they want, and if they can't find them, make them."

Shaw wrote the story Pygmalion from which the play My Fair Lady was adapted. In the play, a wealthy Englishman named Henry Higgins makes a bet with one of his friends that he can transform a young woman living in poverty on the street into a lady who will be accepted in the highest circles of society. Her name is Eliza Doolittle. Higgins has a vision of what Eliza must become in order for him to win his bet. That vision represents his expectation of her.

As the story progresses, Eliza begins to change, but very slowly. Not until she embraces Higgins' vision of her transformation can all the changes necessary for that transformation take place. Higgins' expectation must become Eliza's self expectation.

Explain that, while it is important for others to have expectations of us and to communicate those expectations, it is far more important that *we* have quality expectations of ourselves. Make the following points about self expectations:

- Self expectations act as limits in every part of our lives.
- People seldom exceed their self expectations.
- When self expectations are low, performance is likely to be low.
- When self expectations are high, performance is likely to be high.
- Self expectations (as well as those of others) need to be reasonable.
- Expectations that are unreasonably high lead to disappointment.
- Expectations that are unreasonably low are limiting and also lead to disappointment.

Remind the students that when we fall short of our own expectations, we have an opportunity to examine the reasons and grow from the experience. Offer this example: *Thomas Edison invented the light bulb after hundreds of failed attempts. With each failure, Edison fell short of his self expectation, yet learned from the experience. Years later, Edison said, "I never had any failures ... just learning experiences." He viewed his 'failures' as steps toward success.*

After your introduction, conduct the following series of four Sharing Circles ("When Someone Lived Up to My Expectations," "A Time When I Met or Exceeded My Own Expectations," "A Time Someone Failed to Live Up to My Expectations," and "A Time I Failed to Live Up to My Own Expectations"), which focuses on understanding and developing expectations. The circles may be done as a series (in a single session) or spread out over several meetings and interspersed with other activities. When the students have completed all four Sharing Circles, implement the activity/experience sheet, "Building a Reasonable Expectation."

When Someone Lived Up to My Expectations
A Sharing Circle

Objectives:

The students will:
— discuss the differences between their self expectations and the expectations they have of others.
— describe reasonable and unreasonable expectations.
— understand how expectations shape behavior.

Introduce the Topic:

When others realize the expectations we have of them, their successes not only build our confidence in them, they also reinforce our belief that we can accurately predict what other people are likely to do and how they are likely to behave. Today, we're going to talk about times when we had expectations of others that proved reasonable. Out topic is, "When Someone Lived Up to My Expectations. "

Think of a time recently when you expected someone to behave in a certain way or to achieve something you believed they could achieve. Maybe a friend was getting discouraged over a tough assignment, even though you fully expected that he would succeed and he did. Perhaps you expected your mom to decide to stay in her present job instead of taking a promotion that she didn't really want and she stayed. Or maybe you expected some people to be on time and they were. Whatever it was you expected, the other person delivered. Take a moment and think about an incident like this in your life. Our topic is, "When Someone Lived Up to My Expectations.

Discussion Questions:

1. How do you feel toward someone who meets an expectation you have? How do you feel toward yourself?

2. How does having reasonable expectations of others help build relationships?

3. What has having reasonable expectations of others taught you about yourself?

4. What happens when we have unreasonable expectations of others?

A Time When I Met or Exceeded My Own Expectations
A Sharing Circle

Objectives:

The students will:
— discuss the differences between their self expectations and the expectations they have of others.
— describe reasonable and unreasonable expectations.
— understand how expectations shape behavior.

Introduce the Topic:

Having reasonable expectations of ourselves is a key to developing self confidence and self esteem. Meeting a self expectation gives us a sense of accomplishment, and we can personally acknowledge that we did what we set out to do. Today, we're going to talk about times like this in our lives. Our topic is, "A Time When I Met or Exceeded My Own Expectations. "

Recall a time when you consciously set out to do something and succeeded. Maybe you wanted to create something, like a painting or an original song to play on your guitar. Perhaps you decided to get a good grade on an assignment, or finish a difficult task that had been dragging on for several weeks. Or perhaps you wanted to change something about yourself or your environment. For example, you may have wanted to stop procrastinating. Or you may have wanted to reconcile two friends who had been fighting. Take a few moments and think about it. Our topic is, "A Time When I Met or Exceeded My Own Expectations.

Discussion Questions:

1. *How do you feel when you accomplish something you set out to do?*
2. *What did you learn from your success?*
3. *How does having expectations help us achieve?*
4. *Why is it important that our self expectations be reasonable?*

A Time I Failed to Live Up to
My Own Expectations
A Sharing Circle

Objectives:

The students will:
— discuss the differences between their self expectations and the expectations they have of others.
— describe reasonable and unreasonable expectations.
— understand how expectations shape behavior.

Introduce the Topic:

Throughout our lives, we create mental pictures of what we want to do or what we want to be. Some of these pictures have to do with very significant things, like the grades we expect to get in school or career we expect to choose. Others have to do with simple things, like what clothes we're going to wear or how we're going to approach someone to ask a question. In either case, we mentally rehearse what we believe might happen. Any time we do this, we are creating an expectation of ourselves. Sometimes things work out just as we pictured and we say we have achieved our expectation. Other times things don't work out and we say that we have failed to achieve our expectation. Today, we're going to talk about a time when things did not work out. Our topic is, "A Time I Failed to Live Up to My Own Expectations."

Think of a time when you created a picture in your mind of how you wanted something to be, and it just didn't turn out that way. You may have pictured something you wanted to do or something you wanted to have or become. It may have been something very significant, or it may have turned out to be relatively insignificant, but it was an expectation you had of yourself. Take a few moments to think about this. The topic is, "A Time I Failed to Live Up to My Own Expectations."

Discussion Questions:

1. *How did you feel when you discovered that you had failed to live up to your expectations?*

2. *What did you learn from failing to meet your self expectation?*

3. *What things might make a self expectation unreasonable?*

4. *How do self expectations differ from the expectations we have of others?*

5. *In what ways do our expectations affect the way we behave?*

A Time Someone Failed to Live Up to My Expectations
A Sharing Circle

Objectives:

The students will:
— discuss the differences between their self expectations and the expectations they have of others.
— describe reasonable and unreasonable expectations.
— understand how expectations shape behavior.

Introduce the Topic:

Just as we are always creating expectations of ourselves, we also have expectations of others. And from time to time, we end up being disappointed. Today, we are going to talk about experiences like that. Our topic is, "A Time Someone Failed to Live Up to My Expectations. "

Think of a time recently when someone let you down. You don't have to share something major, just a time when you felt disappointed. Maybe you expected someone to invite you to a party and he didn't. Or perhaps you expected the star player on your team to save the game and she didn't. Your group may have expected leadership from a member who didn't want the responsibility.. Whatever you decide to share, don't name the person, just focus on the difference between what the other person did and what you expected him or her to do. Think about this for a few moments. Our topic is, "A Time Someone Failed to Live Up to My Expectations. "

Discussion Questions:

1. *How do you feel when someone fails to live up to your expectations? How do those feelings compare to the ones you have when you fail to live up to your own expectations?*

2. *What has being disappointed taught you about your expectations of others?*

3. *Who is responsible for expectations and whether they are reasonable or unreasonable?*

4. *How do our expectations of a person affect our relationship with that person?*

Building a Reasonable Expectation
Discussion and Experience Sheet

Objectives:

The students will:

— discuss the differences between their self-expectations and the expectations they have of others.
— describe reasonable and unreasonable expectations.
— understand how expectations shape behavior.

Materials:

the experience sheet"An Expectation I Have" for each student

Directions:

Remind the students that expectations can be either reasonable or unreasonable. Whether for themselves or others, reasonable expectations are more likely to be met than unreasonable expectations.

Point out that one of the universal characteristics of successful people and effective leaders is that they have reasonable and achievable expectations of themselves and others. Suggest that to learn this skill, the students need to really think about expectations when they form them. They may need to take into account many factors in order to decide what is a reasonable expectations in a particular situations. Most people tend to form their expectations without much thought. Successful people and effective leaders take time to develop expectations and in so doing are seldom disappointed in themselves or others.

Pass out the experience sheet, "An Expectation I Have" to each student. When all the students have completed the experience sheet, lead a summary discussion.

Discussion Questions:

1. How do you feel about the expectations you developed?

2. Does having reasonable expectations give you greater confidence? In what ways?

3. How do expectations of others and self-expectations differ? How are they the same?

4. Does having a reasonable expectation of yourself change you? How?

An Expectation I Have
Experience Sheet

We all have expectations of ourselves and others. However, most expectations are not consciously formed. In fact, if thinking is involved at all, it's usually wishful.

Here's your chance to develop four carefully thought out expectations—three for yourself and one for someone else. But before you write down each expectation, ask yourself, "What are the chances that this expectation will be met?" Think about your talents, skills, knowledge, resources, abilities, disabilities — anything that might play a role. Do the same when forming an expectation for someone else. If you see obstacles, ask yourself if they can be successfully dealt with. In short, don't write down an expectation unless you think there is a good likelihood that it will be met.

An expectation I have of myself within the next 24 hours is:

_____

_____

An expectation I have of myself within the next week is:

_____

_____

An expectation I have of myself within the next month is:

_____

_____

_____

Now, think about your friends and other people with whom you associate at school, at meetings, on teams, and at home. Choose one person and carefully form an expectation based on something specific that person is going to do.

What is the person's name?

_____

What is the situation or event?

_____

_____

What is your expectation?

_____

_____

_____

The Importance of Goals
Experience Sheet and Discussion

Objectives:

The students will:
— informally assess their goal setting attitudes and behaviors.
— describe the benefits of setting and achieving goals.

Materials:

a copy of the experience sheet, "Take Charge of Your Life" for each student

Directions:

Pass out the experience sheet to the students. Ask them to answer the questions at the beginning and then read the information on goal setting that follows. When they have completed their sheets, ask if anyone has a goal that he or she would like to share with the rest of the class? When everyone has shared who wants to, lead a discussion using these and other questions.

Discussion questions:

1. *What role do goals play in a person's life?*
2. *How will having goals help you get what you want in life?*
3. *Do people have goals through their whole lives?*
4. *How can setting goals now help you direct your future?*
5. *How do you feel after you have accomplished a goal?*

Take Charge of Your Life
Experience Sheet

Without giving them a lot of thought, quickly answer these questions:

What do you want in life?

_____

_____

_____

What is one goal you have for yourself right now?

_____

_____

_____

Do you feel in charge of your life?

_____

Are you happy with the direction your life seems to be taking?

_____

Why or why not?

_____

_____

_____

Why is setting goals important? Because goals can help you do, be, and experience everything you want in life. Instead of just letting life happen to you, goals allow you to *make* your life happen.

Successful and happy people have a vision of how their life should be and they set lots of goals (both short term and long range) to help them reach their vision. A man named David Starr Jordan said, "The world stands aside to let anyone pass who knows where he is going." You can bet that those people who know where they are going are getting there by setting goals.

When you set goals, you are taking control of your life. It's like having a map to show you where you want to go. Think of it this way: You have two drivers. One driver has a destination (her goal) which is laid out for her on the map. She can drive straight there without any wasted time or wrong turns. The other driver has no goal or destination or map. He starts off at the same time from the same place as the first driver, but he drives aimlessly around, never getting anywhere, using up gas and oil. Which driver do you want to be like?

Winners in life set goals and follow through on them. Winners decide what they want in life and then get there by making plans and setting goals. Unsuccessful people just let life happen by accident. Which do you want to be? You do have a choice. Goals aren't difficult to set—and they aren't difficult to reach. You decide.

3. _____

_____

_____

_____

_____

Do you remember some of the benefits of setting goals? Write down three:

1. _____

_____

_____

_____

_____

2. _____

_____

_____

_____

A Process for Setting and Attaining Goals
Discussion and Experience Sheet

Objectives:

The students will:
— explain that having a goal is the first step to achieving what one wants.
— identify specific steps for attaining goals.
— develop skills in setting practical and achievable goals.
— experience goal attainment.

Materials:

pens or pencils, blank note paper, copies of the experience sheets, "Tips for Setting Goals," "You Can Reach Your Goals!" "Goal Achievement Score Sheet" for each student

Directions:

This is a continuing activity, designed to be used with students over several weeks. It will allow them to experience the satisfaction of setting and achieving goals that are important to them, and will teach them an effective goal setting process.

Introduce the activity. Explain to the students that most successful people have a habit of setting clear goals concerning things that they want to accomplish. Explain that in this activity, the students will set goals and experience the feeling of success that comes with attaining them.

Point out that when we think of goals, we usually picture big, important things like going to college, buying cars and houses, taking vacations, etc., but that we set dozens of smaller goals each day. Ask volunteers to share some of the things they want to accomplish today. Point out that stating these things is the simplest form of goal setting.

Pass out the experience sheets, "Tips for Setting Goals" and "You Can Reach Your Goals!" Review Tips for Setting Goals, offering an example or two to illustrate each point. Then give the students time to complete the first two pages of the experience sheet, "You Can Reach Your Goals!", writing down their goals and answering the questions.

If possible, spend a few moments with each student, reviewing his or her goals to make sure that they are attainable, properly written, and within the purview of the student to achieve (not dependent on events or people outside the student's control).

When the studetns have finished their work, explain that goals are achieved in steps. Success is measured as each step is completed. Point out that The Goal Achievement Score Sheet will help them break down their goals into more easily managed steps.

Allow enough time for the students to write down the steps for each goal. While they are writing, offer assistance. This task will be foreign to most students and they will need guidance in formulating the steps. Again, you can add significantly to this activity by sitting with each student and assisting in the development of the steps particularly if the goal pertains to success in your class.

Explain to the students that you will follow-up with them on a regular basis to see how they are progressing with achieveing their goals.

Direct the students to keep their experience sheets and refer to them daily as they work toward their goals. Review the progress of the students weekly or biweekly in class and have the students record their progress on their Goal Achievement Score Sheet. Lead a discussion after each review.

Discussion Questions:

1. *How do you feel about having completed steps toward your goal?*

2. *If you haven't completed any steps, how do you feel about falling short? What can you do about it?*

3. *If you were the leader of an organization or group, how could you go about helping the members set organizational goals?*

4. *When you need the help of others to achieve a goal, how can you build in that requirement as part of your plan?*

Tips for Setting Goals
Experience Sheet

1. **Goals must be clear and describe exactly what you want or will do.**

2. **Goals must be personal.** They must be about you, not someone else.

3. **Goals must be measurable.** You need to know when you have achieved your goal.

4. **Goals must have realistic time limits.**

5. **Goals must be manageable.** Divide big goals into several smaller, attainable goals or tasks. This will enable you to experience results in a shorter period to time.

6. **Goals must be stated in positive rather than negative terms:** (I *will* do something rather than I *won't* do something.)

7. **Goals must be written down.** People are more likely to achieve goals that are in writing. Written goals can be reviewed regularly, and have more power. Like a contract with yourself, they are harder to neglect or forget.

You Can Reach Your Goals!
Experience Sheet

What are goals?

A goal is an end, home base, the final destination, what you are aiming for. Goals can center on having something—clothes, a car, money—or they can center on achieving—finishing school, going to college, having a career, becoming famous, gaining knowledge and honors.

Short-term and long-range goals

Short-term goals include making phone calls, finishing your homework, cleaning your room, doing your chores, or making plans for the weekend. Long-range goals might include planning a trip for next summer, deciding to go to a trade school, a community college, or a university; saving money to buy something special; or making plans for your future career.

When we write goals in the way described below, we connect with the part of our brain that tells us what we need to do. Have you ever wanted to make something? If you have, you may remember that after you decided what you wanted to make (this was your goal) you started thinking of things you needed to have and/or do in order to attain your goal. You even figured out the order in which the steps needed to be completed. Perhaps you wrote down the steps. The more often you set goals in this way, the more often you get what you want.

Take a look at your goals.

On the following page, take a few minutes to write down some of your goals. Check whether each goal is short-term or long-range, and write in the date by which you plan to accomplish it.

Goals are written in special ways.

They are:
1. Positive (They contain no negative words.)
2. Personal (They're about us, not others.)
3. Written as though they are happening now or have already happened. (Never write them as though they are "going to" happen.)

GOAL #1 _____

_____

____ **Short Term** ____ **Long Range**

Target Date _____

GOAL #2 _____

_____

____ **Short Term** ____ **Long Range**

Target Date _____

GOAL #3 _____

_____

____ **Short Term** ____ **Long Range**

Target Date _____

Answer these questions about each one of your goals:

1. Is this goal one you decided to set, or did someone else influence you to set it?
2. How do you feel about having this goal?
3. Is this a realistic goal for you (one that you can attain)?
4. What frustrations or conflicts were involved in setting this goal?
5. What risks are involved in reaching this goal?
6. With whom did you consult before you decided on this goal?

Describe roadblocks that might interfere with your reaching each goal. List strategies for overcoming each roadblock.

	Roadblocks	Strategies
Goal #1	_____	_____
	_____	_____
Goal #2	_____	_____
	_____	_____
Goal #3	_____	_____
	_____	_____

Goal Achievement Score Sheet

Goal #1

Steps Toward Achieving My Goal:

	Review Date	Step Achieved	Step Not Achieved
1. _____			
2. _____			
3. _____			
4. _____			

Goal #2

Steps Toward Achieving My Goal:

	Review Date	Step Achieved	Step Not Achieved
1. _____			
2. _____			
3. _____			
4. _____			

Goal #3

Steps Toward Achieving My Goal:

	Review Date	Step Achieved	Step Not Achieved
1. _____			
2. _____			
3. _____			
4. _____			

The Value of Rewards
Experience Sheet and Discussion

Objectives:

The students will:
— describe the importance of rewarding themselves for goal attainment.
— write down one reward in connection with each of their goals.

Materials:

a copy of the experience sheet, "A High Five," for each student; each students completed experience sheet, "You Can Reach Your Goals" from the previous activity

Directions:

Introduce the experience sheet "A High Five" by saying something like: *An important and often overlooked element of goal setting is the reward. Rewards should be established during the planning process and should be coupled with both short-term and long-range goals. Rewarding yourself for achieving a short-term goal will give you the motivation you need to continue working toward other short-term as well as long-range goals.*

Anything you enjoy or value can be used as a reward. It doesn't have to be big or expensive. Plan to buy yourself some new music or book, or buy a special treat from your favorite bakery. Rewards, like goals, should be realistic. By choosing a reward that is either unattainable or unaffordable, you will be undermining your ability to achieve the associated goal.

Pass out the experience sheet, "A High Five." Give the students a few minutes to transfer their goal statements from the experience sheet, "You Can Reach Your Goals." Then ask the students to think of a realistic yet desirable reward for each goal. When all of the students have completed the experience sheet, have them break into groups of three to five and take turns sharing their rewards. Allow about 10 minutes for interaction. Then lead a culminating class discussion.

Discussion Questions:

1. *How do rewards help the process of goal setting and attainment?*

2. *What is one reward that you have given yourself in the past for achieving a goal? Did that reward encourage you to pursue more goals?*

3. *What are some distinctions between a reward that you give yourself and one that you get as a natural consequence of achieving a goal, like recognition or a good feeling? Which is more important?*

4. *How can we support each other in achieving our goals?*

A High Five
Experience Sheet

When you have set and accomplished a goal, give yourself a high five! It's time to congratualte yourself and reward yourself, too! Think of one nice thing you can do for yourself when you have achieved each of your goals. Describe it here:

Goal #1:

How I will reward myself:

_____

_____

_____

Goal #2:

How I will reward myself:

_____

_____

_____

Goal #3:

How I will reward myself:

_____

_____

_____

One of My Goals Is...
A Goal Reinforcement Activity

Objectives:

The students will:
— describe a personal goal.
— practice dealing with imagined obstacles to the goal.
— identify steps to attaining the goal.

Materials:

Directions:

Locate an area large enough to accommodate groups of three students, allowing ample space between groups.

Divide the students randomly into groups of three. Have them decide who will be A, who will be B, and who will be C. (If one or two students are left over, you can assign additional C's to some groups.)

Explain the procedure to the students: *Person A, you are the "goal setter, " and will state a goal that you want to achieve. Person B, you are the "discourager. " You will come up with all the problems, obstacles, and roadblocks that could make achieving the goal difficult. Person C, you are the "encourager. " You will offer ideas and solutions for achieving the goal. You will help remove the roadblocks. Offer any good ideas you can think of to help the goal setter be successful. After a few minutes, I'll call time and tell you to switch roles. We will do three rounds, so that everyone can play all three roles.*

Choose two volunteers and demonstrate the rotation process and the goal setter/ discourager/encourager interaction. Provide examples of goal statements, positive statements, and negative statements. Lead the activity through three rounds. Circulate, and encourage the students to play their roles with enthusiasm. After everyone has had a turn in each role, facilitate a class discussion.

Discussion Questions:

1. *What obstacles or roadblocks were mentioned most often?*

2. *What were some of the best solutions offered?*

3. *Why do we have dialogues like this inside ourselves? What purpose do they serve? Who usually wins?*

4. *Do you think this activity will help you accomplish your goal? How?*

Something I Did (or Made) That I'm Proud Of
A Sharing Circle

Objectives:

The students will:
— identify personal accomplishments
— describe the feelings generated by accomplishments.

Introduce the Topic:

Our topic for today is, "Something I Did (or Made) That I'm Proud Of. " We've all done something, or made something, of which we've been proud. Think of an example in your life, and tell us about it. Maybe the thing that comes to mind makes you proud because other people thought well of you for achieving it. Or perhaps your accomplishment is something no one knows about except you. Perhaps you helped someone who really needed and wanted help, and giving that help made you feel proud of yourself. Or maybe you made something like a perfect friend egg, or fixed something, like a machine, and doing that made you feel proud of yourself. Perhaps you mastered a skill that had been eluding you for a long time. Think for a minute and see if you can come up with something. It can be an accomplishment from your childhood or something you've done recently. The topic is, "Something I Did (or Made) That I'm Proud Of.

Discussion Questions:

1. *Who besides yourself was proud of you? How did they show it?*

2. *Why is it important for people to feel proud of themselves?*

3. *Have you ever felt it wasn't good to feel proud of yourself.? If so, what caused you to feel that way?*

4. *How does pride in ourselves help us continue to accomplish things?*

Something I Wish I Could Do Better
A Sharing Circle

Objectives:

The students will:
— identify a specific area in which they would like to improve.
— discuss how to set a goal in their area of improvement.

Introduce the Topic:

The topic for today is, "Something I Wish I Could Do Better. " Few of us are completely satisfied with ourselves. Wanting to improve is a natural part of growing and is a lifelong process. Is there something that you wish you could do better right now? Maybe you'd like to be more comfortable meeting and getting to know other people. Or perhaps you'd like to be a better ball player, or draw and paint with greater skill. You might wish you were better at getting your homework done, or keeping your room clean. Think of ways in which you wish you could improve and select one you feel comfortable sharing with us. Again, the topic is, "Something I Wish I Could Do Better.

Discussion Questions:

1. *How easy or difficult was it for you to share about something you would like to do better?*

2. *Why is it important to target areas for self improvement?*

3. *If you were to set a goal in this area, how would you go about it? How would it help you?*

4. *How can we balance self acceptance and the desire to improve?*

Something I Would Like To Achieve in the Next Three Years
A Sharing Circle

Objectives:

The students will:

— describe a vision of themselves in the near future.

— discuss how goal setting can help them realize their vision.

Introduce the Topic:

The topic for today's Sharing Circle is, "Something I Would Like To Achieve in the Next Three Years. " Think for a moment about yourself right now. Then think of yourself three years from now. What would you like to have, do, or be by that time? Maybe you'd like to become an "A " student, learn a foreign language, study a musical instrument, form a band, start your own savings account, or write a book. You can achieve in any area you choose. Take a moment to think before you share on our topic, "Something I Would Like To Achieve in the Next Three Years.

Discussion Questions:

1. What is an achievement?

2. How often and how well do you set achievement goals?

3. How can setting goals help you direct your future?

Things I Can Do To Get
Where I Want To Be
A Sharing Circle

Objectives:

The students will:
— describe a goal.
— identify steps required to reach the goal.
— explain how planning facilitates goal attainment.

Introduce The Topic:

Today's topic is, "Things I Can Do to Get Where I Want to Be. " The concept suggested by this topic is very important to consider when you want to achieve something. To reach any kind of a goal, it is very important to think of all the steps you will have to take. This is true whether your goal is immediate, like getting a good grade on a test, or long term, like wanting to travel to a foreign country when you get out of school. Whatever it is, you need to be aware of all the things it takes to get what you want.

Think of one of your goals. Now try to picture yourself doing everything necessary to reach that goal. Do you have to learn a new skill or language? Do you have to read books or talk with people in order to get information? Will you have to change your way of thinking, or strengthen your body, or move to another city? This is a complex topic, so take your time. When you're ready to share, the topic is, "Things I Can Do to Get Where I Want to Be. "

Discussion Questions:

1. *Why is it important to be aware of what it takes to reach a goal?*

2. *Although we all shared about different goals, what similarities did you notice in the steps it will take to reach them? What differences did you notice?*

3. *Have you ever faced a task that seemed impossibly difficult, until you broke it down into steps? If so, tell us how that was helpful?*

DECISION MAKING AND PROBLEM SOLVING

Understanding the processes and influences that shape decision making and influence problem solving is a fundamental skill characterizing effective leadership and success in any endeavor. The quality of a decision is frequently determined by the degree of conscious effort that has gone into its making. Good decision making involves using information about values, goals, influences, alternatives, and probable consequences to make choices that achieve desirable outcomes. Problem solving is often a larger process that involves multiple decisions. Leaders must solve problems entailing many decisions on a regular basis, and they must be able to facilitate groups involved in these same processes. Leaders must ensure that decisions and solutions align with a group's visions and goals. If this condition does not exist when matters of inclusion, interdependence, or diversity are considered, normalization is jeopardized and real change precluded.

Activities in this unit ask students to assess previous decisions, and to help each other make current decisions and solve existing problems. In the process, students are guided through step-by-step problem solving and decision making processes.

Decisions, Decisions!
Experience Sheet and Discussion

Objectives:

The students will:
— understand and describe how decisions are influenced.
— develop and practice a process for effective decision making.

Materials:

the experience sheet, "The Decision-Making Process;" whiteboard or chart paper

Directions:

Distribute the experience sheets. Read through the decision making steps with the students, examining each one. Here are some suggestions to discuss and questions to ask:

- **(Step 2)** Knowing what is important to you and what you want to accomplish involves such things as likes/dislikes, values, and interests. Most important, it involves having goals. As the Cheshire Cat said in Alice in Wonderland, " If you don't know where you're going, any road will take you there."

- **(Step 3)** You can get information by talking to people, visiting places, watching TV, exploring the internet, and reading. Once you have the information, you must be able to evaluate it. If two people tell you to do opposite things, how are you going to know which is right? What if neither is right? What if both are right?

- **(Step 5)** Consider the advantages and disadvantages by looking into the future. Ask yourself what would be the probable outcome if you chose each of the alternatives available. Practice with the students by asking them to predict their future based on these questions:

What would happen if:

— you did not go to college?
— you never got married?
— you dropped out of school?
— you became temporarily disabled?
— you became a professional rock singer?
— you decided never to drink alcohol?
— you decided not to have children?
— you became permanently disabled?

How did you make your predictions? What information did you use?

- (Step 6) When you reach the decision point, don't procrastinate. If you've done a good job on the other steps, you can choose the best alternative with confidence. Remember, if you don't choose, someone else may choose for you.

- (Step 7) Not every decision requires an action plan, but the big ones usually do. The decision to attend a four-year college in another state won't come true unless you make it. And that means more decisions. Can you think what they are?

Give the students time to complete the experience sheet.

Have the students choose partners and take turns sharing their decisions and decision making process. Facilitate a culminating discussion.

Discussion Questions:

1. *What did you learn about decision making from this activity?*
2. *What can happen if you put off making a decision?*
3. *Why is it important to know your interests and values when making decisions?*
4. *How can having goals help you make decisions?*

The Decision-Making Process
Experience Sheet

The decision-making process involves using what you know (or can learn) to get what you want.

Here are some steps to follow when you have a decision to make:
1. Recognize and define the decision to be made.
2. Know what is important to you—your values—and what you want to accomplish—your goal.
3. Study the information you have already; obtain and study new information, too.
4. List all of your alternatives.
5. List the advantages and disadvantages of each alternative.
6. Make a decision.
7. Develop a plan for carrying out your decision.

Now let's see how the process really works.
Think of a decision that you need to make in the next month. Define it here:

_____

_____

What is your goal relative to this decision?

_____

What kinds of things that are important in your life (your values) might affect, or be affected by, this decision?

_____

_____

_____

What kinds of information do you have or need?

Things to read:

Things to think about: _____

_____

_____

_____

_____

People to talk to: _____

Things to do:

_____

_____

_____

_____

What are your alternatives and what are the advantages and disadvantages of each?

Alternative	
Advantages	**Disadvantages**
Alternative	
Advantages	**Disadvantages**
Alternative	
Advantages	**Disadvantages**

Decision Point!
Which alternative has the best chance of producing the outcome you want?

Now that you've made a decision, you need to develop a plan for putting that decision into action. Use the space below to describe each step you need to take and when you will do it.

This Is the Plan

Steps: **When?**

1. _____

_____

_____

2. _____

_____

_____

3. _____

_____

_____

4. _____

_____

_____

5. _____

_____

_____

6. _____

_____

_____

_____

Decisions and Outcomes
Assessment and Discussion

Objectives:

The students will:
— understand and describe how decisions are influenced.
— state the outcomes and possible consequences of specific decisions.

Materials:

a copy of the experience sheet, "More About Decisions " for each student; a slip of paper for each student; a coin

Directions:

Begin by defining *decision making* as a process in which a person selects from two or more choices. Point out that:

- A decision is not necessary unless there is more than one course of action to consider.
- *Not* deciding is making a decision.
- Two people facing similar decisions create unique outcomes because they want different things.
- Learning decision making skills increases the possibility that a person can have what he or she wants.
- Each decision is limited by what a person is *able* to do and what he or she is *willing* to do. *Ability* is increased by having more alternatives. *Willingness is* usually determined by values and goals.

Pass out the experience sheet, "More About Decisions." Give the students a few minutes to complete the sheet.

To reinforce the differences between decisions and outcomes, play a game with the students. Introduce the game by saying: *I'm going to play a game of chance with you. You must make the decision whether or not to play. I am going to flip a coin. Before I flip it, I want you to write down on a slip of paper whether the coin is "heads " or "tails. " Put your name on your paper, and give it to me. After I flip the coin, I will go through the papers and give every student who guessed correctly five extra points for the day. Those who guessed incorrectly will get no extra points. Remember, you do no have to play.*

Play the game. Afterwards, ask the students these questions:

— How many chose to play the game?
— How many chose not to play the game?
— If you chose to play the game, but guessed incorrectly, was that a poor decision or a poor outcome? (outcome)
— If you played the game and guessed correctly, was that a good decision or a good outcome? (both)
— If you chose not to play the game, was that a good or a poor decision? Why?

Conclude the activity with further discussion.

Discussion Questions:

1. *What did you find out about your "worst decision" from this activity?*

2. *What is the difference between decisions and outcomes?*

3. *If your decision was truly bad, how could you have made a better one?*

4. *What kinds of decisions require study and thought?*

More About Decisions...
Experience Sheet

Write down all the decisions that you can remember making so far today. For example, you probably made decisions about what to wear, what to eat, how to spend your breaks and with whom. You may have made decisions about whether to go to class, how to approach an assignment, what to say to someone, and whether to tell the truth. Include all types of decisions on your list.

Decisions

1._____

2._____

3._____

4._____

5._____

6._____

7._____

8._____

9._____

Now go back through your list of decisions and code each one with a number from this scale.

0 = I have no control over this type of decision; it is dictated by others.

1 = This type of decision is automatic, routine, or habitual.

2 = I occasionally think about this type of decision.

3 = I think about this type of decision, but I don't study it.

4 = I study this type of decision somewhat.

5 = I study this type of decision a lot.

What does this exercise tell you about how you make most of your decisions?

_____

_____

_____

_____

_____

_____

_____

What is the worst decision you ever made? Write a brief description of it:

_____

_____

_____

_____

_____

_____

_____

Decision or Outcome? Next time you're tempted to kick yourself over a "bad" decision, consider this:

- When you say that a decision is poor, you probably mean the *result* or *outcome* is not what you wanted.

- Good decision making minimizes the possibility of getting bad outcomes, but it doesn't eliminate the possibility.

- A *decision* is the act of choosing among several possibilities based on your judgments.

- An *outcome* is the result, consequence, or aftermath of the decision.

- You have direct control over the decision, but *not* over the outcome.

- A good decision does not guarantee a good outcome, but it does increase the chances of a good outcome.

Go back and look at your "worst" decision again. Was it really a bad decision, or was it a reasonable decision with a bad outcome?

Factoring a Decision
Experience Sheet and Discussion

Objectives:

The students will:
— describe and analyze a recent decision.
— discuss factors that affect decision making.
— explain how to increase alternatives during decision making.

Materials:

the experience sheet, "Increasing Your Alternatives;" whiteboard or chart paper

Directions:

Begin the activity by reviewing concepts related to decision making that were covered in previous activities. Elicit contributions from the students and write notes on the board. Be sure to make the following points:

1. A decision is not necessary unless there is more than one course of action to choose from.
2. Not deciding is making a decision.
3. Learning decision making skills increases the possibility that I can have what I want.
4. Each decision is limited by what I am *able* to do. For example, if I cannot drive a car, I cannot choose between walking and driving.
5. The more alternatives I know about, the more I am *able* to do. For example, if I am unaware of a particular college, I cannot include it among my alternatives when deciding where to go to school.
6. Each decision is also limited by what I am willing to do.
7. What I am willing to do is usually determined by my values, beliefs, preferences, and past experiences.

Pass out the experience sheet, "Increasing Your Alternatives" to each student. Go over the items on the sheet and answer any questions. Then give the students time to complete the sheet.

Have the students form small groups and share their responses. When they have finished, lead a culminating class discussion.

Discussion Questions:

1. *What did you learn about decision making from this activity?*

2. *What can you do to increase your alternatives in a decision making situation?*

3. *What kinds of things determine your willingness to try a particular alternative?*

4. *When your willingness is more a product of low self confidence than of values, how can you overcome that roadblock?*

5. *How do your beliefs affect decision making? Your attitudes? Your previous experiences?*

Increasing Your Alternatives
Experience Sheet

Think of a decision you need to make. Describe it here: _____

_____

_____

What are you able to do in this situation? Write down as many realistic alternatives as you can think of.

_____   _____

_____   _____

_____   _____

_____

Go back and circle all of the alternatives you are willing to try.

One of the best ways to increase your chances of making a good decision is to increase your alternatives. Write down as many ideas as you can think of for increasing your alternatives.

1. _____

2. _____

3. _____

4. _____

5. _____

6. _____

7. _____

8. _____

9. _____

10. _____

Remember: In decision making, information is your biggest ally. Read books, ask questions, or browse the web.

Steps for Solving a Problem
Experience Sheet and Discussion

Objectives:

The students will:
— understand and describe how decisions are influenced.
— develop and practice a process for effective problem solving.

Materials:

the experience sheet, "Steps for Solving a Problem;" whiteboard or chart paper

Directions:

Pass out the experience sheet, "Steps for Solving a Problem." Have the students read each step in the problem solving process with you while writing notes on their sheet. Generate discussion after each step by asking appropriate open-ended questions. Introduce a personal example (a problem that you need to solve) and take it through the process as part of the discussion. If time permits, go back through the process a second time, using as an example a problem described by one of the students.

Discussion Questions:

Stop all blaming

1. What happens when you get bogged down in the blaming game?

2. What are people who constantly blame others for their problems trying to avoid?

3. How is blaming others the same as giving away your power?

Define the problem

1. Why is it so important to know exactly what the problem is?

2. Why does it matter whether it's your problem or someone else's?

3. When should people not be left to solve their own problems?

4. What can happen when a person gets all worked up about a problem that isn't even theirs?

Consider asking for help

1. When is it wise to ask for help?

2. Who gets to decide what kind of help you need?

3. If what you want is information or advice, and instead the person tries to solve the problem for you, what can you do?

Think of alternative solutions.

1. What is the advantage of thinking of alternatives?

2. If you can't think of more than one or two alternatives, what should you definitely do before making a decision?

3. How does collecting information expand your alternatives?

Evaluate the alternatives.

1. What are some ways of collecting information?

2. Why not just do the first thing that comes to mind?

3. Why is it important to imagine what will happen as a result of trying each alternative?

Make a decision.

1 . If you still can't make a decision, which steps in the process could you return to? (2., 4., 5., and 3., in that order. The problem may be incorrectly defined; you may need to gather additional information; the consequences may need further consideration; or help may be called for.)

Follow through.

1. Why stick to a decision?

2. What can you do if the solution doesn't work or more problems come up?

3. How can you evaluate your decision?

4. What's an example of a big problem in our society that used to be a much smaller problem with a relatively easy solution?

Steps for Solving a Problem
Experience Sheet

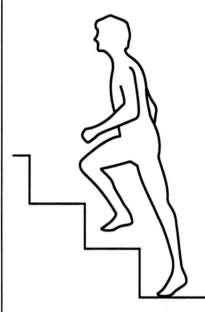

What is a problem?

A problem can be a complicated issue or question that you have to answer. Or it can be something in your life that is causing you frustration, worry, anger, or some other kind of distress. In order to answer the question or get rid of the distress, you must "solve" the problem. Problems often have several parts. Solving the whole problem involves making a series of decisions — at least one decision for each part of the problem.

Next time you are faced with a problem, follow these steps to a solution:

1. Stop all blaming.

It will help me to understand that blaming someone (including myself) for the problem will not solve it. If I really want to solve the problem, I need to put my energy into working out a solution. Blaming myself and others is a waste of time.

2. Define the problem.

Next, I need to ask myself two questions to help me get started. "What exactly is the problem?" and "Whose problem is it?" If I find that it's not my problem, the best thing I can do is let the people who "own" the problem solve it themselves. Or I can ask them, "How can I help you?"

3. Consider asking for help.

Once I'm sure I "own" the problem and know what it is, I may choose to ask someone for help. For example, I may decide to talk over the problem with a good friend, or the school counselor.

4. Think of alternative solutions.

I need to ask myself, "What are some things I could do about this?" I need to think of as many reasonable ideas for solving the problem as I can. To do this, I will probably need to collect some information.

5. Evaluate the alternatives.

Next, for each idea I come up with, I need to ask myself, "What will happen to me and the other people involved if I try this one?" I need to be very honest with myself. If I don't know how someone else will be affected, I need to ask that person, "How will you feel about it if I..."

6. Make a decision.

I need to choose the alternative that appears to have the best chance of succeeding. If my solution is a responsible one, it will not hurt anyone unnecessarily—and it will probably work.

7. Follow through.

After I've made the decision, I'll stick to it for a reasonable length of time. If the decision doesn't work, I'll try another alternative. If the decision works, but causes more problems in the process, I'll start all over again to solve them. And I'll try not to blame myself or anybody else for those problems.

Solving a Current Events Problem
Current Events Research, Brainstorming, and Discussion

Objectives:

The students will:
— select and summarize a current events article dealing with an important issue or event.
— generate solutions to a current events problem presented by the teacher.
— in small groups, achieve consensus on a solution to the problem.

Materials:

current events articles (brought by the students); an article of your choosing to read to the students

Preparation:

Ask the students to find a current events article from a newspaper or news magazine or internet news service and bring it to school on the day of the activity. Require that the articles deal with an issue or event of some importance. **Bring an article of your own dealing with a problem for which creative solutions are obviously needed.**

Directions:

Talk to the students about the importance of being well informed. Explain that the community, the nation, and the world are made up of individuals such as they. The world is shaped by the interest and participation of individual people working together. People build, produce, feed, govern, and educate. In the process, they create conflicts and problems, which they also must solve. Ask the students what kinds of issues, events, and problems they discovered through their news article. Ask two or three volunteers to briefly tell the class about their articles.

Have the students share their article with a partner. Allow about 5 minutes for this. Then read *your* article aloud to the class. Define terms used in the article, and discuss the problem. Ask these questions:

— *What is the problem?*
— *Whose problem is it?*

Announce that through group discussion, the students are going to come up with solutions to the problem described in the article you just read. Have the students form groups of three to five. Give them I minute to choose a leader and a recorder. Then announce that the groups will have 10 minutes to brainstorm solutions to the problem.

Call time after 10 minutes, and have the groups discuss and evaluate their suggestions, one at a time. Their task is to choose one solution to present to the class. Suggest that they answer these questions:

— *Will this solution solve the problem?*
— *Can this solution actually be done?*
— *Will combining any suggestions make a better solution?*

Allow a few more minutes for discussion. Urge the groups to use the process of consensus seeking to make their decision. Have the group leaders report to the class. Then lead a culminating discussion.

Discussion Questions:

1. *What was the hardest part about finding a solution to this problem? What was the easiest part?*

2. *If your group was not able to come to a decision, why not?*

3. *How were disagreements or conflicts handled in your group?*

4. *Is there any way for individuals or nations to avoid having problems? Explain.*

5. *How will learning to solve problems here in the classroom help prepare us to solve them in the outside world? ...in college? ...in a career?*

Have a Heart!
Decision Making Exercise

Objectives:

The students will:
— make a shared decision concerning a difficult issue.
— describe their shared decision making process.
— describe how values and attitudes affect decision making.

Materials:

one copy of the "Patient Waiting List" for each small group; writing materials

Directions:

Announce that the students are going to have an opportunity to make group decisions concerning a highly charged, imaginary situation in which individual values and attitudes may play a significant role.

Ask the students to form groups of five to seven. Give each group a copy of the "Patient Waiting List," and suggest that every group choose a recorder.

Read the situation and the list of patients to the groups:

Situation:

You are surgeons at a large hospital. Your committee must make a very important decision. Seven patients need a heart transplant. There is only one heart donor at this time. All of the patients are eligible to receive the heart. All are physically able. And all have compatible blood and tissue typing. Which patient would you choose to receive the heart? Why? Your committee must agree on the choice.

(Be sure to acknowledge that most recipients of organ transplants are now managed by a nationwide computer network, which largely removes such difficult decisions from the hands of the surgeons themselves. Ask the students to participate as if such a system had not yet been developed. Also, remind the students that patients who do not receive this heart will not *automatically* die. Some (not all) will probably survive until another donor is available.)

Refrain from giving any further instructions or suggestions. Allow at least 20 minutes for decision making. Then reconvene the class and question each group about its decision and its decision making process. Facilitate discussion.

Discussion Questions:

1. *What was your decision?*

2. *How did you arrive at your decision.*

3. *What decision making method did you use (consensus, voting, etc.)?*

4. *How was your decision influenced by your values? ... your attitudes? ... your prejudices?*

5. *Who provided leadership in your group?*

6. *How were disagreements and conflicts handled?*

7. *How satisfied are you with your own level of participation in this exercise?*

Patient Waiting List.

- 31 year old male; Black; brain surgeon at the height of his career; no children

- 12 year old female; Vietnamese; accomplished violinist, blind

- 40 year old male; Hispanic; teacher; two children

- 15 year female; White; unmarried; 6 months pregnant

- 35 year old male; Hispanic; Roman Catholic priest

- 17 year old female; White; waitress; high school dropout; supports/cares for a brother who is severely disabled

- 38 year old female, White, AIDS researcher, no children, lesbian

I Didn't Want to Have to Make a Decision
A Sharing Circle

Objectives:

The students will:
— identify factors that hinder decision making.
— describe strategies that aid decision making.

Introduce the Topic:

Sometimes we're faced with decisions that we don't feel prepared to make. One frequent reason is that we don't have enough information. Another is that we're not sure of our goals. Sometimes we're afraid of the consequences of a decision. Today, we're going to talk about times like this and how we handled them. Our topic is, "I Didn't Want to Have to Make a Decision. "

Think of a time when you didn't feel ready to make a decision. Perhaps a friend asked you to go somewhere and you weren't sure that you wanted to, but didn't want to say no, either. Maybe you were offered a job, but needed more time to decide if it was the best thing for you to do. Or maybe you were buying someone a present and had to decide between two items that you liked equally well. Have you ever had to decide between two answers on a test just as time was running out? Have you ever had to choose which puppy or kitten to give away and which to keep? Take a few moments to think about it. If you decide to share, describe the situation and how you resolved it. The topic is, "I Didn't Want to Have to Make a Decision.

Discussion Questions:

1. *How did you feel when you realized you needed to make a decision?*

2. *How do you feel about your decision now?*

3. *What are some possible consequences of continually postponing a decision?*

4. *When is it legitimate to delay a decision?*

5. *If you have all the necessary information and still can't decide, what can you do to help yourself?*

When I Shared in Making a Decision
A Sharing Circle

Objectives:

The students will:
— describe their contributions to shared decisions.
— describe processes by which shared decisions are made.

Introduce the Topic:

Today's topic is, "When I Shared in Making a Decision. " We all like to be part of the decision making process. We want to help our families plan vacations and decide what movies to see. We want to be involved when our friends decide how to spend Saturday afternoon. When a decision involves us, we want to express our ideas and give our input.

Tell us about a time when you helped make a group decision. You and some friends may have made a joint decision regarding an activity or project. Perhaps you helped make all the decisions required for a holiday or birthday surprise. Right now, you and your parents may be deciding which college you should attend, or what color the house should be painted. It doesn't matter if the decision was big or small; we want to know how you felt and what you learned from the experience. The topic is, "When I Shared in Making a Decision. "

Discussion Questions:

1. *What are the advantages of helping to make decisions that affect you?*

2. *Can you describe the process that you and your companions went through when making your shared decision?*

3. *What do you usually contribute to the decision making process? What do you count on others to contribute?*

4. *How do you feel when you are a part of the decision making process?*

I Had a Problem and Solved It
A Sharing Circle

Objectives:

The students will:

— describe a real problem and how they solved it.

— recognize their ability to solve problems.

— describe strategies for solving problems.

Introduce the Topic:

Problems are something we all have throughout life. It's not possible to live without problems, but it is possible to solve them. Which brings us to our topic for today, "I Had A Problem and Solved It. "

Think of a problem that you experienced, and solved, in the recent or more distant past. Maybe it had to do with a class, a requirement for graduation, or some extra support you needed at school. Perhaps the problem was associated with a close friendship, or was centered around your home life. If you choose to share, describe the problem, how you solved it, and the feelings you had when you managed it successfully. Our topic is, "I Had a Problem and Solved It.

Discussion Questions:

1. *What were your feelings while you were working on the problem?*

2. *How can we learn to approach problems as challenges rather than threats?*

3. *What are some problem solving strategies that you heard mentioned today?*

A Problem I'd Like Suggestions
for Solving
A Sharing Circle

Objectives:

The students will:
— describe a real problem and practice listening to the suggestions of others.
— develop and practice a process for effective decision making.

Introduce the Topic:

Sometimes when people offer advice, it can be a real pain, especially if the advice isn't asked for. On the other hand, some decisions and problems are difficult to handle alone. By asking for help, we can multiply our alternatives and thus our chances of making a good decision. Today, we're going to have an opportunity to do just that in the circle. The topic is, "A Problem I'd Like Suggestions for Solving. "

A suggestion is an idea that can be either accepted or rejected. However, when you ask for a suggestion, you are indicating that your mind is "open " and that you will at least consider the idea that is offered. Today, we're going to allow any person who wants to, the opportunity to share a problem. Choose a problem that you need to solve, or a decision that you need to make, for which you'd be willing to consider some suggestions. We'll start with one person sharing a problem; then others may offer alternatives for him or her to consider. Please don't comment on whether or not you think a suggestion will work. Simply acknowledge each suggestion by thanking the person who gave it. If you give someone else a suggestion, keep in mind that the person may not, in the final analysis, use it. One last thing: If your problem involves other people, please don't mention their names. The topic is, "A Problem I'd Like Suggestions for Solving.

Discussion Questions:

1. *How do you feel about accepting suggestions from others?*

2. *How do you react when someone gives you unsolicited advice?*

3. *Why is it often difficult to ask for help?*

4. *What can you do if you think you have valuable information for someone who is struggling with a decision or problem, but you have not been asked for help?*

5. *Under what circumstances should you get involved even if you have not been invited to?*

COOPERATION AND TEAM BUILDING

Knowing how to work with others and to be a contributing member of a team are important skills for both college and career success as well as being primary attributes of effective leaders.

Effective teams are characterized by interdependence and inclusion. Members are valued for their uniqueness. They trust one another, turn to each other for help and advice and, when they experience conflict, utilize positive methods to resolve it. Through activities that promote cooperation and team building, young people acquire many insights and skills necessary to interact effectively with their peers and others, to handle conflict, and to participate productively in collaborative projects and tasks. Teams are distinguished from groups by a team identity that transcends the simple sum of group members. Team members contribute uniquely to that identity. One of the key ingredients characterizing successful teams is trust.

The effective leader knows how to use communication skills to develop trust and to frame clear pictures of the purpose for which the team has been organized. Successful teams have well defined visions to describe their purpose and its related outcomes. The activities in this unit help students assess the qualities and functioning of successful teams, understand how teams are developed, how teams make decisions, how individual behaviors of team members contribute to or detract from teamwork, and recognize that the most common arena in which today's and tomorrow's leader will function is the team.

What's Your Preference
Alone or Together.?
Team Experiment and Discussion

Objectives:

The students will:
— demonstrate the power of team efforts.
— describe advantages of working with a team. ...of working alone.
— identify their preferred way of working, alone or with a group.

Materials:

a stop watch or watch/clock with a second hand; whiteboard and marker; writing materials for each student

Directions:

Have the students form teams of four or five. From the following list, select one word for each team. Write the assigned words on the board so all of the groups can see their word.

identification
reverberation
heterogeneous
responsiveness
haberdasher
refrigeration
significantly
predetermination
simultaneous

Explain to the students that, working individually, they are to write as many words as they can, using the letters in the word that has been assigned to them. Go over the rules, saying: *There will be NO talking. You must write real words of two or more letters using only the letters in the assigned word. For example, if your assigned word contains only one "a, " then new words you come up with must contain no more than one "a. " However, you may use the "a" in more than one word. You will have 5 minutes to come up with as many words as possible.*

Call time at the end of 5 minutes. Explain to the students that in the second round of the activity, they are to follow the same rules, however, this time they will be working together as a team and can talk with each other. Assign each team a new word from the list. Again, allow 5 minutes for brainstorming as many words as possible and then call time.

Poll the teams to find out how many words they came up with while working alone and how many they came up with working as a team. (Chances are the team efforts produced more words.) Hold a culminating discussion. Encourage the students to hypothesize as to why they obtained the results they reported.

Discussion Questions:

1. *How did you feel when you were working alone?*

2. *How did you feel when you were part of a team?*

3. *Under which circumstances, alone or with a team, did you produce more words? Under which circumstances did you enjoy yourself more?*

4. *Why do team efforts often produce better results than individual efforts?*

5. *If you prefer working with a team, what are some things you can do to make yourself more effective when you work alone?*

6. *If you like to work alone, what are some things you can do to be more effective when you are part of a team?*

Stepping Stones
Group Task and Discussion

Objectives:

The students will:
— work cooperatively in teams to solve a problem.
— identify effective and ineffective team behaviors.

Materials:

nine baseball bases (or any suitable substitute, such as cardboard squares or flattened paper bags) to be used as "stepping stones" and a playing area (lawn, gym, or multipurpose room) at least 37 1/2 feet long.

Directions:

Measure off 37 1/2 feet and mark both ends of the playing space. Group the class into teams of no more than ten and no fewer than seven each. (For example, 31 students could be divided into three groups of eight and one group of seven.) Adjust the length of the playing space and the number of stepping stones to accomodate the actual number of players on each team. Allow *one less* stepping stone than there are team members, and subtract 2 1/2 feet from the length of the space for every team member *less than ten,* as follows:

9 members = 35 feet   8 members = 32 1/2 feet   7 members = 30 feet

Explain to the students that you would like them to imagine that between the two markers there is a raging river. Their task is to get each team member across the river, using the bases as stepping stones. As each team attempts to cross the river, members must decide how to use their stepping stones to best advantage. This task involves trial, error, and team cooperation. Team members will need to experiment and help one another.

While the first team attempts to cross the river, the other teams should go to another room so that they cannot watch. This will allow each team to approach the problem without having seen another team work on it. On the other hand, do allow teams that have completed the task to watch the next teams attempt it. Laughter and encouragement on the part of observers will make the activity fun and interesting, but do not allow students to make derogatory statements or sounds.

Discussion Questions:

1. *What was the toughest part of this exercise for you? ... the most enjoyable part?*

2. *How did you work together? Did a leader emerge? How were problems resolved?*

3. *What did your team do that proved particularly effective? ... ineffective?*

4. *What did you see another team do that seemed particularly effective? ... ineffective?*

5. *What did you learn about teamwork from this activity?*

Becoming a Team
Presentation, Role Play, and Discussion

Objectives:

The students will:
— identify four stages of group development.
— describe the characteristics of each stage.
— evaluate the development of a real life group.

Materials:

a copy of the experience sheet, "Becoming a Team" for each student; whiteboard and marker or chart paper and markers

Directions:

Begin by asking the students to help you define the word *team*. Say to them: Six *students who sit at different desks, work on individual assignments, and receive separate grades are not a team. However, when they sit around a table and work on a project together, they start to become a team.*

Try to reach consensus on a definition. For example: A team is a group of people working together, or doing some activity together.

Ask the students to imagine a scenario with you. Say to them: *Suppose I call six of you aside and tell you that you are now the official tutoring team for the class. All students occasionally need extra instruction, and your job is to figure out ways to find out who needs help, and how help should be provided. I want you to get started right away. Do you become a team instantly? No. You have to **develop** into a team. Along the way, you will probably go through several stages.*

Choose six volunteers to play the part of the tutoring team. Have them act out the stages of group development as you present them.

Explain the following stages, one stage at a time. Make notes on the board. Then have the actors role play that stage. (Coaching suggestions are in italics.) Stop the action after 2 or 3 minutes and go on to the next stage.

STAGES OF GROUP DEVELOPMENT

STAGE 1: The team looks for leadership and directions. *You look at each other and ask, "What are we supposed to do?" You feel somewhat confused. Maybe you ask your teacher for help, but for the most part, you realize you're on your own.*

STAGE 2: The team starts to organize. *Conflicts emerge and are settled. You try to figure out all the different parts of the job. For example, you have to decide how to identify students who require extra help, how to equitably distribute tutoring responsibilities among team members, what kinds of training tutors need and how they will receive it, etc.. In the process of getting organized, you sometimes disagree about who should do things and how they should be done.*

STAGE 3: Information flows freely and members feel good about the team. *The team is organized and conflicts are settled. You find yourselves working together extremely well.*

STAGE 4: The team can solve problems. Members are interdependent. *The team seems to be able to tackle anything. Creative ideas are abundant. Members work alone, in pairs, or as a total group with equal success. Every member of the team is valued and is depended upon by every other member.*

Pass out the experience sheet, "Becoming a Team." Go over the directions. Emphasize that many groups never achieve team status because their development stops at an early stage. For example, at Stage 2, some groups are plagued by multiple disagreements and conflicts which are never fully resolved. Allow the students about 20 minutes to complete their sheet (or assign it as homework). Have them share their completed sheets in small groups before leading a culminating class discussion.

Discussion Questions:

1. *Why do groups have to develop?*
2. *What kinds of things might help a group move to higher stages?*
3. *What kinds of things might slow a group down or prevent its development?*
4. *What happens when a group can't get past stage one? ... stage two?*
5. *What stage of development did the real life team you wrote about reach? On what did you base your conclusion?*

Becoming a Team
Experience Sheet

Teams are never created instantly. They have to evolve. As a group works together, it goes through certain stages of development—much like a child goes through different stages as he or she grows up.

STAGES OF GROUP DEVELOPMENT

STAGE 1:
The team looks for leadership and directions.

Members look at each other and ask, "What are we supposed to do?" They feel somewhat confused. Maybe they ask their teacher or boss for help. At some point, however, they realize that if they're going to be a team, they have to start acting like one.

STAGE 2:
The team starts to organize. Conflicts emerge and are settled.

How do members act like a team? Well first, they have to figure out all the different parts of the job. They have to answer the "who," "what," "when," "where," and "how" questions that are part of getting organized. In the process, members sometimes disagree about who should do things and how they should be done.

STAGE 3:
Information flows freely and members feel good about the team.

By the time it reaches this stage, the team is organized and conflicts have been settled. Members find themselves working together extremely well. They still disagree sometimes, but now conflicts are seen as natural and members have found effective ways to resolve them.

STAGE 4:
The team can solve problems. Members are interdependent.

At this stage, the team seems to be able to tackle anything. Creative ideas are abundant. Members work alone, in pairs, or as a total group with equal success. Every member of the team is valued and is depended upon by every other member.

Think of a group or team to which you have belonged. It can be an athletic team, a club, or a group of friends. Reread the "Stages of Group Development" while remembering your group or team. Then carefully answer these questions:

1. Name of the group:

_____

2. Purpose/goal of the group:

_____

_____

_____

_____

_____

_____

3. What stage of development did the group reach?

_____

_____

4. What specific incidents and/or group behaviors support your conclusion? Describe at least three here:

1._____

_____

_____

2._____

_____

_____

3._____

_____

_____

The Team and Me
Self Assessment and Dyad Discussion

Objectives:

The students will
— evaluate their personal behavior in a team situation.
— write a goal for improving their team behavior.
— describe steps for achieving their goal.

Note: This experience sheet is designed to help students evaluate their individual behavior during the "Team Problem Solving" activity; however, it may be used in conjunction with any team or group activity in which they have participated.

Materials:

one copy of the experience sheet, "The Team and Me," for each student

Directions:

Pass out the "The Team and Me" experience sheet. Say to the students: *Think about a recent situation in which you were a member of a team or group. Read through the list of behaviors and decide which ones you are doing about the right amount of, which ones you would like to do more of, and which ones you would like to do less of. Make a check in the appropriate column after each item. Complete Part 1 only at this time.*

Circulate and offer assistance as needed while the students complete the self assessment. When they have finished, ask the students to discuss their self evaluations with a partner. Suggest that they skip any items that they are not comfortable sharing.

Still working with a partner, have the students complete Part 2 of "The Team and Me." Ask them to write down one goal for improving their team behavior. Urge the students to commit to working toward that goal over the next few weeks. Lead a follow-up discussion.

Discussion Questions:

1. *What did you discover about yourself by completing the self assessment?*
2. *What are some behaviors you need to do less of? ... more of?*
3. *What goal did you set for improving your team behavior or skills?*
4. *How do you plan to go about achieving that goal?*
5. *What are your greatest strengths as a team member?*
6. *How can knowing how to be an effective team member help you in school? ...in college? ...in a career?*

The Team and Me
Experience Sheet

Self-Assessment

PART 1:

Think about your behavior in a recent group or team situation. Read through the list and put a check in the appropriate column after each behavior.

	About right	Need to do more of	Need to do less of
Communication Skills			
1. contributing to group discussions			
2. listening actively			
3. inviting others to speak			
4. staying on the topic			
5. interrupting with your own ideas			
Leadership Skills			
6. sharing a vision of the future			
7. giving directions and information			
8. inspiring/encouraging others			
9. demanding you know the right way			
10. pitching in and helping others			
Problem-Solving Skills			
11. stating problems and goals			
12. asking for ideas and opinions			
13. offering your own ideas			
14. evaluating ideas			

	About right	Need to do more of	Need to do less of
Team-Building Skills			
13. demonstrating commitment to group			
14. expressing appreciation of others			
15. helping achieve consensus/agreement			
16. helping to reduce tension			
17. helping to resolve conflicts			
Expressing Feelings			
18. telling others what I feel			
19. disagreeing openly			
20. being sarcastic or putting others down			
21. expressing humor			
Getting Along with Others			
22. competing to outdo others			
23. dominating the group			
24. including others			
25. criticizing others			
26. helping others			
27. being patient			

Part 2:

How do you want to improve your group skills or behaviors? Develop a goal in one area and write it here:

My goal is to..._____

_____

My Favorite Team
A Sharing Circle

Objectives:

The students will:
- — describe the importance of teamwork to accomplishing group goals.
- — describe qualities and behaviors that contribute to effective teamwork.

Introduce the Topic:

Today we're going to talk about teams and the qualities that seem to make them successful. Our topic is, "My Favorite Team. "

Think of your favorite team and tell us what it is and why you like it. Maybe your favorite team is one to which you belong, such as a school athletic team, cheer leading team, chess team, or a project team in one of your other classes. Or perhaps your favorite team is a professional baseball, football, soccer, or hockey team. You can choose a team that exists today, or one that you belonged to when you were a child. You can also describe any group of people that acts like a team, even though the group isn't usually called a team. Tell us what you think makes your team a good team. You might want to mention what the team has accomplished, or describe how individual members of the team contribute to its success. Think about it for a few moments. The topic is, "My Favorite Team. "

Discussion Questions:

1. *What is a team?*
2. *What did most of the teams we mentioned have in common?*
3. *Must a team have a purpose or goal? Why or why not?*
4. *How are teams usually organized?*
5. *What are some of the qualities of a good team member?*

A Role I Play in Groups
A Sharing Circle

Objectives:

The students will:

    identify specific roles they play in group situations.

    describe how the roles played by individuals can help or hinder a group's progress.

Introduce the Topic:

Today, we're going to talk about some of the things we typically do and say in group situations. The topic is, "A Role I Play in Groups. "

We all have many different roles in life. We are children to our parents, role models to our younger brothers and sisters, students at school, and employees at our jobs. In group situations, we take on still other kinds of roles. These roles are often related to what we want to see happen in the group. For example, if you want everyone in a group to be happy, you may play the role of "Harmonizer. " If you enjoy making decisions, you may take on the role of "Leader. " If you are in a bad mood, you may become the group's "Antagonist. " Are you usually quiet in groups? Are you a person who asks lots of questions? Do you tend to clown around a lot? Recall a group you were part Of recently, or a club whose meetings you attend, and tell us about your role in that group. Remember that some people change their role from group to group and from meeting to meeting, while others gravitate toward the same role in nearly all situations. Think about it quietly for a few moments. The topic is, "A Role I Play in Groups.

Discussion Questions:

1. *Why do people play different roles in groups?*

2. *What determines whether a role is "good" or "bad?"*

3. *In what kind of situation would the role of Clown be helpful to a group?*

4. *In what kind of situation would the role of Harmonizer not be helpful to a group?*

5. *How can you become more aware of the roles you play in groups?*

6. *If you don't like a role you often play, how can you change it?*

We Used Teamwork to Get It Done
A Sharing Circle

Objectives:

The students will:
— describe a real situation in which a goal was attained through teamwork.
— identify characteristics of a functioning team.
— describe the effects of teamwork on individual commitment and motivation.

Introduce the Topic:

Today, we're going to talk about teamwork and what it can accomplish. Our topic is, "We Used Teamwork to Get It Done. "

Think of a situation in which you worked with a team of people to accomplish a goal. You can share something about a team activity in which you've participated here in class, or some other team experience you've had recently. Perhaps you belong to an athletic or debate team that won a competition. Maybe your family worked as a team to clean up the house or hold a yard sale. You may belong to an advocacy group that worked to get a law passed or a program started Or you and some friends may have done something together, like cook a meal, plan a party, or hold a car wash. Tell us what the team was trying to accomplish and how you felt being part of it. Take a few moments to think about it. The topic is, "We Used Teamwork to Get It Done."

Discussion Questions:

1. *How did most of us feel about being part of a team?*

2. *What makes a team work well together?*

3. *How does the saying, "The whole is more than the sum of its parts," apply to teams?*

4. *How does working with a team on a school assignment affect the quality of your work?*

5. *How does it affect your motivation?*

6. *How would you characterize the differences between a group and a team?*

7. *How can knowing how to work well in a team help you in college? ...in your career?*

LEADING AND FOLLOWING

Leaders and followers are inseparably connected. To be a leader requires the acknowledgment, acceptance, and affirmation of followers. Many individuals who occupy positions of leadership are not really leaders because they fail to gain the affirmation of those who should be their followers. Leadership is manifested through vision and inspiration; through giving directions and information, supporting and encouraging, participating, delegating, and demonstrating commitment.

In order to accomplish great things, leaders also need to know how to identify those qualities and traits in others that are important to achieving desired outcomes. They need to know how to recruit and organize individuals in ways that produce results. Once they bring people together, they need to inventory skills and organize resources in the most effective ways. Leaders ought to know how to conduct meetings and secure needed information, manage time, develop plans, and direct people and events in ways that produce positive results. The most effective leaders also know how to solicit and utilize feedback to improve performance.

Sometimes leadership is just being there, day in and day out over the long haul. The activities in this unit enable students to assess the avenues and styles through which they provide leadership to others, and to recognize the types of leaders they need when they are followers in specific situations. Various power bases are examined as sources of a leader's influence over others. Using a behavioral lens, leadership is viewed more as a process than a person. The overriding message of this unit is that, depending on the situation and their behaviors, all young people can be and are leaders.

Leaders Are Remembered
for Their Decisions
Research and Discussion

Objectives:

The students will:
— identify and evaluate decisions made by historical or contemporary leaders.
— differentiate between decisions based on established convictions/philosophies and those based on research and study.

Materials:

reference materials such as biographies, history books,, and recent news magazines both online and in print

Directions:

Tell the class about a well known historical or contemporary leader, describing some of the person's better known decisions. Tell the students as much as you can about what went into making the decision. Or, provide the students with details and clues concerning each decision and ask them to guess what it was and who the leader was. Discuss the importance of specific decisions made by leaders throughout history and how those decisions affect people today

Tell the students that you would like them to select a living or historical leader who interests them, and research that leader's life to find out about at least one key decision he or she made that affected the lives of many people. Ask the students to see if they can determine whether the decision was the result of careful study, a preexisting conviction or philosophy of some kind, or both. Suggest that the students not overlook the possibility that the decision was irresponsible, impulsive, irrational, or the result of a plan to satisfy selfish motives.

Give the students several days to research and write their reports. Then ask them to share their findings with one another in triads or small groups. After the small group sessions, conduct a class discussion.

Discussion Questions:

1. *Which decisions were made as the result of careful study, which grew out of a preexisting conviction or philosophy, and which were probably based on both?*

2. *What do we mean when we say a leader "stands for something"?*

3. *How do some of these decisions affect us today?*

4. *Do you think these leaders realized at the time how important their decisions were to the lives of others? Explain.*

5. *Which decisions do you most admire and respect?*

6. *Which decisions seemed wrong, foolish, or irresponsible?*

7. *Which decisions do you think were the toughest ones to make?*

How I Influence Others
Creative Writing and Discussion

Objectives:

The students will;
— define influence and describe how it relates to leadership.
— describe one or more ways in which they influence others.

Materials:

writing materials; art supplies (optional)

Directions:

Introduce the activity by talking with the students about the concept of *influence*. Ask the students to help you brainstorm ideas related to influence. Facilitate a wide ranging exploration of the concept. Write key terms and phrases on the board. Here are some possibilities:

- Influence is often subtle.
- Influence is a form of power.
- The ability to influence is one of the main qualities that defines a leader.
- People who are popular and/or admired have influence.
- Sources of influence include peers, parents, teachers, role models, idols, and advertising
- Groups and crowds influence by sheer numbers.
- People are influenced both consciously and unconsciously.
- Influence often occurs by example.
- Many people aren't aware of how much influence they have.
- Most decisions are based on an interplay of influences.

Tell the students that you'd like them to explore some of the ways they influence other people. Explain that they can fulfill the assignment by writing a story, poem, essay, or short play, or by creating a cartoon. Suggest that they use one of the topics provided, or develop their own.

List the following topics on the board:

Ways I've Influenced Others
How I Got Someone to Change an Opinion
Everybody Started Feeling the Same Way I Was Feeling
How I Got a Person to Stop Doing Something
I Put Pressure on Someone
I Set an Example for Someone Younger Than Me

Allow ample time for the students to work on the assignment. Follow your preferred editing/rewriting procedure.

Invite volunteers to share their finished stories with the class. Identify the types, qualities, and targets of influence in each example and discuss the results. When the sharing is complete facilitate a summary discussion.

Discussion Questions:

   1. *What have you learned about influence from this assignment?*

   2. *What have you learned about your ability to influence?*

   3. *What determines whether or not you can influence someone?*

   4. *How does knowing about influence help you accept or resist it in someone else?*

Styles of Leadership
Presentation, Experience Sheet, and Discussion

Objectives:

The students will:
— define leadership as a process and a shared responsibility in most groups.
— identify five styles of leadership and describe how they work.
— describe circumstances under which different leadership styles are needed.

Materials:

whiteboard and marker; a copy of the experience sheet, "What's Your Style?" for each student

Directions:

Begin by writing the following statement on the board:
Leadership is a process, not a person.

Ask the students what they think the statement means. Facilitate a discussion about leadership and what leaders do. Be sure to make these points:

- Every group/team needs leadership.
- Leadership does not necessarily mean "a" leader.
- In many groups, leadership is shared.
- A leader influences other members of the group/team.
- A leader gets the team, or individual members of the team, to do things that move the whole team in the direction of its goal.

Point out that just as there can be several leaders, there can also be several kinds of leadership. Write the following list of terms on the board:

Providing leadership by...

1. giving directions and information
2. giving encouragement and praise
3. participating and facilitating
4. delegating
5. offering vision and inspiration

Pass out the experience sheet, "What's Your Style?" and ask the students to read the scenarios in Part I with you. After each reading, ask the students to identify (from the list) the type of leadership that is being provided in the scenario. Take a few minutes to discuss each style of leadership. Ask the students to recall times in their own lives when they as followers would have benefitted from that style.

Now give the students a few minutes to complete Part 2 of the experience sheet. When they are finished, lead a culminating class discussion.

Discussion Questions:

1. *What style of leadership do you think you are best at providing?*

2. *What style(s) do you seem to have trouble providing?*

3. *How would you like to improve your own leadership ability?*

What's Your Style?
Experience Sheet

Part 1: Put a ✔ beside the style of leadership being provided in each situation.

The student council decides to sponsor an in-school campaign to promote the concept of a fully integrated school in which all students are included, academically and in student government and activities. Brian, the student body president, appoints Leon and Jackie, both art students, to develop some ideas for a logo and posters. He asks Josh to approach the school newspaper about the idea of doing a series of articles. And he appoints Robin and Sheila to work with Tom and Cindy on an overall plan, including some special "events."

Brian is providing leadership by...

____ giving directions or information.

____ giving encouragement, support, or praise.

____ pitching in, participating, or facilitating.

____ delegating (turning a job over to someone who can do it well).

____ providing vision, creativity, or inspiration.

The school newspaper decides to put out a special edition devoted to the integration theme. Maria, Chris, and Jim are writing the stories. They want to use correct terms and inoffensive language when writing about people with disabilities, but don't have any experience in that area. Ms. Jones, their teacher, gives them a printed summary of the Americans with Disabilities Act, and arranges for Cindy and Tom to come in and advise the entire newspaper staff concerning language and other things they should know.

Ms. Jones, Cindy, and Tom are providing leadership by

____ giving directions or information.

____ giving encouragement, support, or praise.

____ pitching in, participating, or facilitating.

____ delegating (turning a job over to someone who can do it well).

____ providing vision or inspiration.

Robin and Sheila are getting ready to videotape a public service announcement for the campaign. The room and the lights are ready, the actors are there, and the camera operator is waiting for directions, but Robin and Sheila are having a disagreement about which of two scripts to use. They don't have time to rehearse and tape both, and there are real differences between the two. Time is wasting. Tony, one of the actors, starts asking questions that get Robin and Sheila to clarify the pros and cons of each script. Before long, they come to an agreement.

Tony is providing leadership by:

___ giving directions or information.

___ giving encouragement, support, or praise.

___ pitching in, participating, or facilitating.

___ delegating (turning a job over to someone who can do it well).

___ providing vision or inspiration.

Carlos decides to run for junior class president. He has the backing of many students, and they help him put together a well-organized campaign. The student council decides to sponsor a panel discussion among all the candidates for class office. Carlos, who has a speech impairment, uses graphic symbols and gestures to help him communicate. He's very reluctant to be on the panel, because he thinks none of the students in the audience will understand him. Richard, the moderator, tells him, "Carlos, we need you. If you can make *me* understand, you can make *anyone* understand. This is no time to back off!" Richard checks with Carlos daily, answering his questions and concerns, right up to the morning of the event.

Richard is providing leadership by:

___ giving directions or information.

___ giving encouragement, support, or praise.

___ pitching in, participating, or facilitating.

___ delegating (turning a job over to someone who can do it well).

___ providing vision or inspiration.

PART 2:

What's *your* style? Write about some of your leadership experiences below. Remember, someone takes the lead almost every time two or more people get together.

Think of a time when you were aware that a person or group was in the dark about what to do. So you gave them directions or information. Maybe you walked them step-by-step through the task. Write about it here:

_____

_____

_____

Now write about a time when someone was discouraged or insecure about his or her ability to accomplish something. You knew the person could do it, so you offered him or her lots of encouragement and praise—and it worked!

_____

_____

_____

_____

_____

Describe a time when you observed that a project or activity was bogged down, so you jumped in and helped out, and got it going again.

_____

_____

_____

_____

Describe a time when you recognized that something needed to be done, so you found someone who could handle the job, and asked that person to take over.

_____

_____

_____

_____

Write about a time when you had an idea or vision of something that you wanted to have happen. By sharing your vision with some other people, you motivated them to help. Eventually, your dream became reality.

_____

_____

_____

_____

188

The Power to Lead
Experience Sheet and Discussion

Objectives:

The students will:
— define power as a source of influence over others.
— identify seven bases of power and explain how they work.
— assess their own power bases in specific leadership situations.

Materials:

a copy of the experience sheet, "Who Has Power?" for each student; whiteboard or chart paper

Directions:

Begin by writing the word *power* on the board. Ask the students what it means to them. Generate discussion by asking such questions as, "Who has power?" and "What do we mean when we say that someone is a powerful person?" Jot down ideas that the students contribute, and at some point offer this dictionary definition:

Power: *the possession of control, authority, or influence over others.*

Pass out the experience sheet, "Who Has Power?" Ask the students to read through Part 1 of the sheet together, discussing the different power bases and brainstorming additional examples of each one. In the course of the discussion, make these points about power.

- We all have power.
- Power is like energy. It enables us to accomplish things.
- Having power is not bad. Only the *misuse* of power is bad.
- Power is what enables a leader to influence others.
- A leader may gain power from several different sources.
- The kind of power a leader has depends on the *perceptions* of his or her followers. A supervisor may think that she is popular and well liked by her workers, but if the main thing keeping the workers in line is fear of losing their jobs, the supervisor's personality is *not* her main source of power.
- When you are providing leadership to others, ask yourself what enables you to influence them. What are your power bases? Try to figure out how your followers see you.

Give the students a few minutes to complete Part 2 of the experience sheet. Stress that *any* situation in which they provided leadership to others is acceptable for the purpose of completing this assessment. They do not have to be student council president or captain of the football team. When the students have finished, ask them to form triads and share their self assessments with two other students. Reconvene the entire group to lead a culminating discussion.

Discussion Questions:

1. *What did you learn about yourself from this activity? What did you learn about power?*

2. *How did power get a bad reputation? Why are some people afraid of it?*

3. *Who determines what kind of power a leader has, the leader or the follower? (the perceptions of the follower)*

4. *How will you use this information when you are a leader?*

Who Has Power?
Experience Sheet

PART 1

Who has power? Practically everyone. Every time you influence the behavior of another person, you are doing so out of some type of **power base**. Leaders certainly have power—influencing others is their main job. To understand power better, read through these descriptions. Think of at least one person you know who has each kind of power. (Keep in mind that some people possess several types of power.)

Power Bases:

Punishment Power is based on fear. People follow this type of leader because failure to do so might result in some type of undesirable consequence, such as an unwanted work assignment, criticism, a bad grade, or getting fired. Parents, teachers, law enforcement officers, principals, and bosses all have punishment power—but *only* if others believe they will use it.

Connection Power is based on the leader's "connections" with influential or important people—important to the follower, that is. The follower hopes to meet, please, or become close to one of these "important" people *through* the leader. An example of someone with connection power is the personal secretary to the boss, or the best friend of someone you want to date.

Expert Power is based on what a person knows. A leader with expert power has skills or knowledge that others need to do their jobs. Followers allow this leader to influence their behavior because they respect him or her. Doctors have a lot of expert power.

Information Power is based on the leader's access to information that others see as valuable. This person doesn't have to *understand* the information (that's expert power), only have access to it . This power base influences others because they need the information or want to be "in on things." A librarian is an example.

Position Power is based on the leader's job title. The higher the position, the more the power. A leader with position power influences others because they believe the leader has the official "right" to direct their activities. The president of an organization and the chairperson of a committee have position power.

Personal Power is based on the leader's traits, personality, or character. A leader with personal power is generally liked and admired by others. People *want* to be associated with this leader and follow him or her enthusiastically.

Reward Power is based on the leader's ability to reward others. Parents, teachers, principals, and bosses all have reward power, too, because they can give recognition, good grades, promotion, love, and/or money.

PART 2

What kinds of power do you have? Think
of a leadership position you have held.
Ask yourself, "Why did others follow
my lead?" Think about it for a moment,
and then rank the following statements in
order of their accuracy (1 through 7).

They followed me because:

___ I could punish them if they didn't cooperate with me.

___ I had connections with influential and important persons.

___ They respected my understanding, knowledge, judgement, and experience.

___ I had access to information that was valuable to them.

___ My position gave me the authority to direct their activities.

___ They liked me personally and wanted to do things that would please me.

___ I could reward and support them if they cooperated with me.

Holding Your Own With Authority Figures
Small-Group Brainstorming and Discussion

Objectives:

The students will:

— identify distinct models of authority that they are likely to deal with in their lives.
— describe appropriate ways of approaching and responding to different authority models.

Materials:

whiteboard, chart paper, and colored markers

Directions:

Preparation: With a colored marker, write across the top of a sheet of chart paper, "Approaching Authority Figures." Divide the paper in half by drawing a line down the middle. Label the left column "Authority Models" and the right column "Approach Skills." As the activity develops, you may need to use additional sheets of paper.

Introduce the activity by saying in your own words: *When I say the words "authority" and "authority figure," what picture comes into your mind? Think for just a few moments of all the people who have had authority over you throughout your life ... now think of other authority figures whom you may encounter in the future.*

Ask the students to name some of the authority figures in their lives, and to predict future authority figures. Jot suggestions on the board. Expect the students to mention parents, teachers, religious leaders, doctors, police, bosses, legislators, etc.

Explain to the students that these people represent social models with distinct types of authority. In your own words, elaborate: *If a person is conversing in Russian and her companion insists on responding in French, communication is seriously jeopardized. If a dancer starts doing the waltz and his partner responds with the cha cha, not only will the movements of the dancers be totally uncoordinated, the two will probably step all over each other. Communicating with an authority figure works along the same lines. If you are able to identify the authority model or style you're dealing with and have the skills to initiate interaction and respond appropriately, you will be much more likely to have an impact and accomplish your goals.*

Inform the students that to heighten their awareness concerning appropriate approach and response modes, they are going to work in small groups to brainstorm the skills necessary to successfully deal with a particular authority model, and contribute their findings to the chart which you have started.

List several authority models in the left column of the chart. Use these examples and add others that you feel are appropriate:

- parental/family
- law enforcement
- military
- community leaders
- religious

- school
- medical
- welfare
- corporate
- political

Choose one authority model, and list several appropriate approach and response skills in the adjacent column. For example, the skills necessary to respond to a political authority figure might include, organizing, letter writing, persistence, patience, controlling emotions, and the ability to discern and follow a chain-on-command. Skills for the parental/family model might include respect, affection, incentive, obedience, and cooperatien.

Divide the class into equal groups and assign each group one model of authority. Or you may choose to let each group select its own. Give the groups 10 minutes to come up with a list of three to six key skills for approaching and responding to that type of authority figure.

Have each group report its list to the entire class. After the list is read, invite discussion and input from the class. Try to reach consensus on the final list of skills for the chart. Have a representative from the group write the list of skills in the second column of the chart adjacent to the authority model. Follow the same procedure for each group. Then have a volunteer read the chart to the class in its entirety to determine if any item needs to be added or deleted. Ask the students to summarize their learnings about the concept of authority models in a culminating discussion.

Discussion Questions:

1. *Why is it important to be able to identify the model of authority you're dealing with?*

2. *What are some of the skills necessary to communicate successfully to different models of authority?*

3. *What could happen if you always responded the same way, regardless of the authority model?*

4. *How might the manner in which you respond to authority create conflict?*

5. *If you frequently find yourself responding inappropriately to authority, how can you change that pattern?*

Excuse me, Ms. Mayor...
Open-ended Role Play

Objectives:

The students will:
— practice effective techniques for communicating with persons in authority.
— identify individual patterns of dealing with authority.

Materials:

one copy of the scenarios list for each student; the chart developed during the activity, "Holding Your Own With Authority Figures;" any props that the students wish to use to enhance their scenarios

Directions:

Remind the students of the concept of authority models/styles (introduced in the activity, "Holding Your Own With Authority Figures"). Tell them that practicing effective techniques for dealing with persons in authority can help them successfully meet their goals as leaders and agents of change. Suggest that one of the best ways to practice is to act out impromptu scenarios, using the appropriate skills.

Distribute the list of scenarios. Explain that the scenarios are open ended, i.e., the behaviors required are not described. The task of the students is to think of appropriate approaches and responses and act them out. Post the chart from the previous activity and suggest that the students refer to it throughout the role plays.

Choose volunteers to perform the first two or three role plays in front of the class. Then, to maximize individual practice, have the students form smaller groups. Suggest that students take turns acting out the authority figures and the young adults in the scenarios, in order to experience both points of view. Circulate and coach the groups. Lead a culminating discussion.

Discussion Questions:

1. *Which authority figures did you most enjoy playing? ... least enjoy playing?*

2. *Which authority figures did you have difficulty approaching or responding to? Which were easier? Why?*

3. *What happened when you communicated inappropriately with an authority figure?*

4. *By communicating inappropriately, do you diminish a person's authority in any way? Explain.*

5. *Why is it important to practice a variety of skills, even though some of them may not be to your liking?*

6. *How can you learn more about successful interaction with authority figures?*

Scenarios

- You are having a meeting and the landlord comes to the door complaining about the noise.

- You approach your church minister (rabbi, priest, elder, etc.) on behalf of a friend with a severe disability who has repeatedly requested an opportunity to assist with services.

- You have just joined the Navy and your commanding officer tells you to pour some coffee and, by the way, you certainly are nice to look at.

- Your parents oppose your becoming involved in a political action group and you discuss it with them.

- Your grandfather has a big van and you want him to transport some students to a leadership camp in the mountains and stay on as a participant.

- You think the aisles at the gift shop where you work are too narrow for people with wheelchairs, and you approach your supervisor about it.

- You are questioned by a police officer concerning a peaceful demonstration you are leading.

- You approach the principal for permission to organize and stage a rally at noon on the school grounds.

- You go to court to testify on behalf of a friend who is from a minority group who has filed a suit against her employer alleging discrimination.

- The principal sees you putting up posters in the courtyard when everyone else is in class and you must explain why you are there.

- You have been working as a wrapper in a fast-food restaurant for several months. Now you have a new supervisor who continually criticizes the way you wrap the burgers.

- You and a group of students approach the mayor asking for support and funding for a Youth Leadership Day you are organizing to promote full inclusion and integration.

- At your job in the Post Office, a fellow worker with more seniority lets you do all of the clean up before leaving, even though you are still recovering from cancer surgery.

Managing Time
Discussion and Experience Sheet

Objectives:

The students will:
— evaluate their use of time.
— identify time wasters and ways to reduce or eliminate them.
— explain the relationship between time management and goal attainment.

Materials:

the experience sheet, "Control Your Time;" for each student

Directions:

Begin by reminding the students of the importance of goals. After reviewing some of the concepts they have discussed concerning setting and attaining goals, point out that one of the hardest things about attaining goals particularly long-range goals is making the time to do what's needed to reach them.

In your own words, explain: *Most of us are pretty good at reaching short-term goals. We do it every day. One reason is that short-term goals usually have short-term deadlines. For example, if you don't make that phone call this afternoon, you won't know if your plans for tomorrow are on or off. If you don't finish your homework early, you won't be able to watch TV. If you don't repair your bike before the weekend, the Saturday morning ride is off.*

Long-range goals often don't have deadlines at all. At least not at first. Instead, they require careful planning and the completion of lots of small tasks. Going to Europe after graduation, for example, involves earning and saving money, making travel arrangements, getting a passport, deciding where to go, what to see, how to travel, where to stay, and whom to go with, just for starters. A long-range goal without a plan is just a dream.

Try to get in the habit of writing down all the steps required to reach a goal. Then start taking those steps right away. Even if your goal is five years down the road, there are things that you can do about it now! Getting control of your time will allow you to take daily, weekly, or monthly steps toward your long-range goals.

Pass out the experience sheet, "Control Your Time" to each student. Review the directions and make sure all the students understand how to create the "Day Pie."

Give the students a few minutes to complete the experience sheet. Then have the students form small groups and share their "day pies," and identified time wasters. Suggest that the groups generate additional ideas for controlling and eliminating time wasters. Conclude the activity with a class discussion.

Discussion Questions:

1. *What did your "day pie" tell you about the time you spend doing various things?*

2. *What changes would you like to make in your use of time?*

3. *What were the biggest time wasters in your group?*

4. *Which ideas for reducing or eliminating time wasters are most likely to work for you?*

5. *What have been the biggest time wasters in organizations and groups to which you've belonged?*

6. *If you were the leader of an organization, what could you do to help manage the group's time well and reduce time waste?*

Control Your Time!
Experience Sheet

Make a "Day Pie."

Estimate how many hours or parts of hours you spend in school, sleeping, doing homework, engaged with social media, earning money, eating, watching TV, playing, reading, working, and other things. Use the blank "Day Pie" chart on the page following the list of "time-wasters" below to record how you spend your time. Divide your "day pie" into slices that represent how much time you spend doing each thing during 24 hours. Label each slice. Once you've completed the pie, take a good look at it.

Are you satisfied with how you spend your time?

Where can you fit in the steps you must take to reach your long-range goals?

Control time-wasters.

It has been said that, "You waste your time whenever you spend it doing something less important when you could be doing something more important." *Do you agree with that statement? Why or why not?*

To determine whether or not an activity is a time-waster for you, measure it against your goals. Is the activity helping you reach your goals? If not, how can you reduce or eliminate the time you devote to it?

Put a ✔ beside your time-wasters.

___**Telephone or Texting.** If you are frequently interrupted by phone calls and text messages while studying or working on an important project, try asking your friends to contact you at an agreed-upon hour. Set aside a special time each day to make phone calls. Limit each call to a few minutes.

___**Television.** It's okay to watch your favorite shows, but don't watch TV just to fill (or kill) time. Instead, use that time to do something that will move you in the direction of a goal!

___**Social Media.** How much time do you spend just checking in or posting?

___**Cluttered room, work area, or desk.** How much time do you waste looking for misplaced items? Not very many people can do their best work amid disorganization. Take some time to "shape up" your space. Have at hand all necessary tools and materials. For studying, you'll need such things as books, paper, pens, pencils, calculator, notebooks, notes, erasers, dictionary, software, and any assistive devices you use.

___**Socializing.** Being with friends is important, but try not to let socializing distract you from other things that you've decided to do. When you plan your day, allow ample time for enjoyable interaction with friends and family. Then, when it's time to work on other goals, don't socialize.

___**Poor communication.** If you frequently fail to understand your assignments, misinterpret statements made by friends or family, or have trouble getting your own ideas across, put some extra effort into communicating effectively. Over 90 percent of all communication is spoken. That means you need to 1) state your own thoughts accurately and clearly, and 2) listen actively and attentively. Phrase your ideas in two or three different ways until you are certain others understand them. When listening, paraphrase what you've heard (restate it in your own words) or ask questions to ensure understanding.

___**Lack of planning.** Always write down your goals, assignments, appointments, chores, and job schedule. Then work out a weekly plan and follow it. With a plan, you'll never have to waste time wondering what to do next.

___**Poor study habits.** Here are some tips: Study at a desk or table. List your assignments in the order in which you plan to do them. Complete your most difficult assignments first while you are alert. Study without interruptions (texts and phone calls) and distractions (TV or radio). Take frequent short breaks. As you read, write down questions that cross your mind. Ask those questions in class or discuss them with a friend. Periodically study with a classmate. Complete reading assignments before they are discussed in class.

___**Procrastination.** Most of us tend to put off things that are unpleasant, things that are difficult, and things that involve tough decisions. These are often the very things that contribute most to our success! Try these procrastination cures:

• Do unpleasant tasks first. Or do them in small pieces, setting a deadline for each.

• Break down difficult tasks into smaller parts. Keep breaking down the parts until you see the first step.

• Break down difficult tasks into "mini-jobs." Make each mini-job small enough to finish in less than 10 minutes.

• Get more information. A task may seem difficult simply because you don't know enough about it. The more you know, the more likely you are to become interested and involved.

Create Your Own Day Pie

Discover how you spend your time. Then decide if you are satisfied with how you're spending your time.

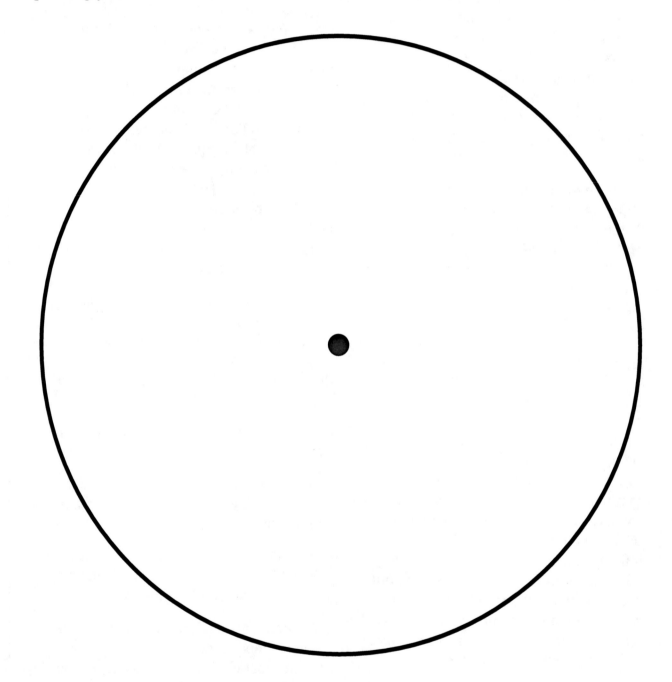

Now, decide how you are going to fit in the steps you must take to reach your long range goals.

How To Lead an Effective Meeting
Brainstorming, Experience Sheet, and Discussion

Objectives:

The students will:
— establish criteria for effective meetings.
— identify steps that a leader can take to ensure that meetings work.

Materials:

the experience sheet, "A Meeting of Minds;" whiteboard; chart paper and marking pens for each small group; masking tape

Directions:

Begin by asking the students to comment on any meetings they have attended lately. In particular, get them to focus on how well the meetings were run. Using the board, begin jotting down positive comments. Without restricting or overly directing the discussion, gradually develop a list of criteria for effective meetings. As the discussion subsides, go back over the criteria and add any from the following list that are missing.

Criteria for Effective Meetings

1. Adequate preparations are made.
2. Group members help set the goals and agenda for the meeting.
3. Everyone takes responsibility for ensuring that the group sticks to the agenda and accomplishes its goals.
4. The leader moves things along at a comfortable pace.
5. A record is kept of what happens at the meeting.
6. Group members evaluate how well they have met their goals.
7. Plans are made for follow-up action.

Have the students form groups of five to seven and choose a recorder. Distribute the chart paper and marking pens. Tell the groups that their task is to take each criterion from the board, and brainstorm a list of things that they, as leaders, need to *know* or to do in order to satisfy that criterion and have an effective meeting.

Allow about 15 minutes for brainstorming. Then have the recorders tape their lists on a wall or bulletin board. Compare and compile the lists, and use them to generate discussion. Fill in with items from the following list that have not been covered:

What I as a leader need to know:

- When to hold a meeting and when not to.
- What the goals of the meeting are.

- Who I want to attend and why.
- What kind of involvement and participation I want.
- What size of meeting I want.
- What type of meeting I want.
- Where I want to meet.
- How much time I am going to allow for the meeting.
- What roles I want participants to play.
- What kind of record I am going to keep.
- Who the recorder will be.
- Techniques for involving people.
- How to facilitate discussion.
- How to mediate conflict.
- Who has the power to make final decisions.
- What decision making method the group will use (voting, consensus, etc.).

Pass out the experience sheet, "A Meeting of Minds," to the students. Go over the "Twenty Steps to a Successful Meeting." Ask the students to imagine themselves going through the steps in preparation for a meeting. Facilitate discussion.

Discussion Questions:

1. *Why is it important to give people an agenda in advance?*

2. *What kinds of room setups encourage participation?*

3. *What can you do if only a few people are there when the meeting is supposed to start? How can you handle late arrivals?*

4. *Why is it important to let people help set the agenda?*

5. *How can you get people to focus on one thing at a time, so that discussion doesn't jump all over the place?*

6. *What can you do if one person dominates discussion?*

7. *What are some ways of evaluating a meeting?*

8. *Why send a follow-up memo to everyone?*

9. *How do you feel about your ability to lead a meeting?*

Extension:

Develop a series of simulated meetings and have students take turns leading them. Encourage the leaders to satisfy as many of the criteria for effective meetings and to practice as many of the steps for leading successful meetings as possible. Choose a different student to act as recorder during each meeting. Act as a coach to everyone—leader, recorder, and participants.

A Meeting of Minds
Experience sheet

Getting ready to call a meeting? Want it to be successful? Then follow these...

TWENTY STEPS TO A SUCCESSFUL MEETING

Before the meeting:
1. Plan: *Who?, What?, When?, Where?, Why?, How many?.*
2. Prepare and send out a tentative agenda in advance.
3. Have the room set up.

At the beginning of the meeting:
4. Start on time.
5. Call the meeting to order.
6. Go over the agenda, make any changes, and finalize.
7. Make sure everyone knows what his or her role is.
8. Set time limits.
9. Review any tasks that were supposed to have been completed since the last meeting.

During the meeting:
10. Get everyone to focus on the same problem in the same way at the same time.
11. Have a recorder keep a record of what happens, preferably on chart paper so everyone can see it.
12. Encourage everyone to participate.
13. Facilitate discussion and decision making.

At the end of the meeting:
14. Clarify what needs to be done: *Who?, What?, When?, etc.*
15. Set a date and place for the next meeting and develop a tentative agenda.
16. Evaluate the meeting.
17. Close the meeting in a positive way.
18. Clean up and rearrange room.

After the meeting:
19. Prepare a memo to group members, summarizing decisions made at the meeting.
20. Follow up on action items and begin to plan the next meeting.

Facilitating Discussions
Experience Sheet and Group Practice Sessions

Objectives:

The students will:
— practice facilitating group discussions.
— discuss and demonstrate specific facilitation techniques.

Materials:

the experience sheet, "Keep 'Em Talking!;" whiteboard or chart paper

Directions:

Begin by pointing out that one of the most important jobs of a leader is to facilitate discussions concerning decisions that must be made, problems that must be solved, and issues, projects, and events that a group is considering.

Explain that the job of a leader/facilitator is to keep the discussion focused on the topic, clear up anything that seems confusing, and create an atmosphere where everyone can participate in a cooperative manner.

Pass out the experience sheet, "Keep 'Em Talking!" Go through the guidelines for facilitating discussions and discuss each item briefly. Act out some of the suggestions in an impromptu fashion, involving various members of the class.

Divide the class into two or three smaller groups and ask the groups to cluster their desks or chairs in different corners of the room. On the board, list several topics for discussion, such as:

- A School Rule That Needs to Be Changed
- Achieving Positive Interaction Among All Students and Groups on Campus
- Opening Up Cliques and Promoting Inclusion
- A New Kind of Special Event on Campus
- A Problem on Campus That Needs to Be Addressed

Select a leader for each group by asking for volunteers or playing a game of chance (e.g., drawing straws). Have the groups choose a topic for discussion from the board (or substitute one of their own) and participate in a 10-minute discussion. Sound a warning after 8 minutes, wait 2 minutes, and then call time. Choose new leaders, and direct the groups to hold a second 10-minute discussion. Repeat the process at least once more. Reconvene the class and lead a culminating discussion.

Discussion Questions:

1. *How did you get your discussion going? How did you keep it going? How did you close it?*

2. *What was the easiest part about leading a discussion? ... the hardest part?*

3. *What kinds of problems did you have and how did you resolve them?*

4. *How did you handle uncooperative group members?*

5. *How well did you do at getting everyone to participate?*

6. *How will you use what you learned from this activity?*

Keep 'Em Talking!
Experience Sheet

The word facilitate means "to make easier." That's what a leader does when he or she facilitates a discussion. The leader makes it easier for people to express their ideas and make decisions. When you facilitate a discussion, keep these tips in mind:

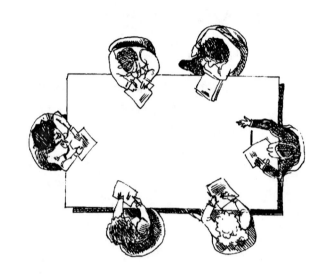

To get a discussion started:

1. Make sure everyone knows what the discussion is about and what the reason for having it is.

2. Don't be too directive. You want others to take the lead, too.

3. Be a model. Demonstrate the kind of participation you want from others.

4. Use questions to get the discussion started. For example, ask, "How do you feel about this problem?"

5. Have a recorder write things down on a board or sheet of chart paper so that everyone can see as well as hear the ideas that are expressed.

6. Relate the discussion to what's actually going on in members' lives. They'll participate more enthusiastically if they can see how the topic affects them.

7. Use humor to break tension or boredom.

8. Allow your own leadership style to come through.

To keep a discussion going:

1. Give everyone an equal chance to participate.

2. Stay on the subject.

3. Model active listening.

4. Clarify by restating the contributions of others.

5. Summarize by pulling together various parts of the discussion and summing them up.

6. Keep the pace moving so people don't get bored or feel their time is being wasted.

7. Help group members work well together. Promote cooperation and positive interaction. Deal with conflict constructively and fairly.

8. Be aware of what's happening in the group. Watch for signs of restlessness that might mean people are bored, confused, or tired. Long silences could mean the same things. Notice eye contact and body posture, too.

9. When expressing your own opinion, use "I" messages. Say, "I think . . ." or "It seems to me that..."

10. Talk directly to people, never about them.

11. Avoid asking questions that call for "yes" and "no" responses. They do nothing to stimulate discussion. Instead, ask open-ended questions such as, "What are your ideas about this project?"

To close a discussion:

1. Give people a warning. Say, "Just a couple of minutes left on this topic."

2. Ask someone to summarize important points and decisions.

3. Announce what the next steps are, and/or when the topic will be discussed again. Review assignments. Make sure everyone knows what he or she is expected to do.

Giving and Receiving Feedback
Experience Sheet and Discussion

Objectives:

The students will:
— practice a process for giving and receiving constructive feedback.
— identify opportunities for giving and receiving feedback.

Note: Use this activity as an immediate follow up to some other activity involving group participation. For best results, implement with students/groups who have worked together long enough to feel comfortable with, and trusting of, one another.

Materials:

the experience sheet, "What Is Feedback?"; whiteboard or chart paper

Directions:

Write the term feedback on the board and ask the students to explain what it means. Jot suggestions on the board and use them to spark discussion. At some point, compare the students' ideas to this dictionary definition:

Feedback: *the return of evaluative or corrective information about an action or process*

Ask the students if they can see how the ability to give and receive feedback benefits a leader. Make these points and solicit other benefits from the students:

- Giving and receiving feedback is a form of sharing.
- Feedback helps us see ourselves more clearly.
- Feedback helps us to change our behaviors and those of others.
- Feedback tells us how we affect others.
- Feedback encourages honesty and builds trusting relationships.
- Feedback allows us to learn and to consider new viewpoints.

Announce that the students are going to practice giving each other feedback. Have them rejoin the groups in which they participated during the previous activity (the one for which this activity is serving as a follow up). Then, in your own words, explain: You are going to give each other feedback about your participation in the previous activity. Each person will have a turn being the Receiver. The Receiver always speaks first, saying what he or she likes and wishes to improve about his/her own participation. Then other members of the group take turns giving feedback to the Receiver.

Pass out the experience sheet, "What Is Feedback? Discuss the guidelines one at a time. Write the steps in the feedback process on the board. Go through them one at a time.

Steps in the Feedback Process:

1. Receiver shares how he or she feels about own participation.
   a. in general
   b. strongest point.
   c. one thing that can be improved.

2. Group members take turns briefly stating:
   a. one thing they like about the person's participation and want to see continue.
   b. one way (if any) they think the person can improve.

3. Person listens to feedback without attempting to explain, make excuses, or discount positive feedback. Questions for clarification are okay.

Ask a student to help you demonstrate. Model the process by giving that student feedback on something you have observed him or her doing recently. Be sure to observe the guidelines in your demonstration.

Have the students practice giving and receiving feedback in their groups. Allow sufficient time for every group member to receive feedback. Then reconvene the class and facilitate a discussion. Emphasize that feedback does not have to be formalized the way it was in this activity. Often, two or more people agree to give each other feedback privately and informally.

Discussion Questions:

1. *How did you feel when you were giving feedback? ...receiving feedback?*

2. *What is the easiest part of giving feedback? ... the hardest part?*

3. *How much difficulty did you have as a Receiver accepting constructive criticism without defending or explaining yourself?*

4. *Was it hard to receive positive evaluations without discounting them? Why?*

5. *In what kinds of situations could you use the feedback process? How would it help you in those situations?*

What Is Feedback
Experience Sheet

Feedback helps people change and grow. A leader occasionally needs to give feedback to someone in the group. A leader should also be open to receiving feedback from others.

Feedback Is...

• descriptive, not judgmental.
Describe what you see, without attaching labels to it. For example, say, "I like the fact that you rarely miss a meeting," instead of, "You're very dependable." Or say, "You interrupted me twice and John once," instead of, "You're rude."

• specific, not general.
Tie your comments to something specific that you saw. For example, instead of saying, "You never listen," try saying, "When we were making assignments during the meeting, I had to repeat yours three times."

• informing not commanding.
This is the same as using "I" messages. Say, "I haven't finished yet," rather than, "Stop interrupting me."

• about behaviors which can be changed.
Don't use feedback to remind people of something over which they have little or no control. For example, don't tell a person with a speech impairment that he or she is hard to understand.

• asked for, not imposed.
Before giving a person feedback, ask for permission. For example, say, "I have some reactions to your presentation. Would you like to hear them?" Remember to ask for feedback, yourself. Say, "I'd like to hear from anyone who has a suggestion about how I could do a better job."

• well timed.
The best time to give or get feedback is usually as soon as possible after the incident in question. But first be sure that both people want to do it.

• checked to ensure accuracy.
To make sure you heard it correctly, restate any feedback given to you . When you *give* feedback, you can ask the receiver to do the same.

How to Receive Feedback:

• Just listen.

• Don't explain.

• Don't make excuses.

• Don't discount compliments or other positive feedback.

• Ask questions only if you don't understand something.

• Say, "Thank you" or "I appreciate your feedback."

• Remember, you have a choice: You can accept the feedback and work on changing your behavior, or you can reject the feedback and decide not to change your behavior. However, keep your decision to yourself.

A Leader I Admire
A Sharing Circle

Objectives:

The students will:
— identify a leader whose accomplishments they respect and admire.
— describe qualities and skills associated with leadership.
— state that the primary condition defining a leader is the willingness of people to follow.

Introduce the Topic:

Today we're going to talk about people in leadership positions whom we admire because of the way they carry out their responsibilities. Our topic is, "A Leader I Admire."

The person you choose to talk about could be your own age like the president of a student organization or the captain of a team. Or he or she could be an adult with a responsible leadership position in business or government. Maybe you think the President of the United States or the leader of some other nation is doing a particularly admirable job. Or maybe you feel a deep respect for a certain member of Congress or a local leader, such as the mayor. On the other hand, the leader you admire could be closer to home. Your parents, for example, are the leaders of your family, and the principal is the leader of this school. If you have a part-time job, keep in mind that your boss is the leader of everyone who works for the company. Regardless of whom you choose, tell us what you admire in this person. What effective leadership qualities and skills does he or she demonstrate? What has he or she accomplished? Why do people willingly follow this leader? Think about it for a few moments. Our topic is, "A Leader I Admire.

Discussion Questions:

1. *What similarities did you notice in the qualities these leaders possess?*

2. *Is it possible to be a leader without the cooperation of followers? Under what circumstances are people forced to follow someone they don't admire?*

3. *Are leaders born or developed? If developed, how?*

4. *To become an admired leader, what's one skill or quality you would need to develop?*

A Time When I Was the Leader
A Sharing Circle

Objectives:

The students will:
— describe a time when they provided leadership to others.
— identify leadership qualities and behaviors in the context of specific situations.

Introduce the Topic:

Our topic today is, "A Time When I Was the Leader." Most of us have had one or more experiences with leadership or being in a position of authority. Yours may have been very brief, or you may have had an official leadership position that lasted several months. There are many ways of providing leadership. Maybe you found yourself confronted with an emergency and had to take charge. Or perhaps you were the head of a team or study group, or supervising some small children. Maybe you were on an athletic team that wasn't doing very well, so you gave everybody a pep talk. Have you ever realized that your club or team needed some equipment or refreshments and sent someone off to get them? Have you ever stood up in a bogged down meeting and suggested what the group should do next? These are all examples of leadership.

Being the leader usually means that you can and do influence the other members of the group to do certain things. When you were the leader, how did you use that power? Were you assertive? Were you aware that you were influencing others? If so, how did that make you feel? Think about it for a few moments. The topic is, "A Time When I Was the Leader."

Discussion Questions:

1. *What do you like most about being the leader? What do you like least?*

2. *What is the difference between a leader using his or her influence and someone using peer pressure?*

3. *When you are the leader, how do you react when a member of your group doesn't want to do things your way?*

4. *What does it take to be a leader?*

5. *If more people assumed leadership more often, how would we benefit?*

6. *When is it a good idea to have one designated leader?*

A Time Someone Misused Power
A Sharing Circle

Objectives:

The students will:
— relate examples of the misuse or abuse of power.
— describe possible causes and consequences of power misuse/abuse.

Introduce the Topic:

Power in itself is neither good nor bad. What we do with power is what counts. We can use our power to lead others responsibly and accomplish great things, or we can use our power in destructive ways. Today, we're going to take a few minutes to talk about the negative use of power. Our topic is, "A Time Someone Misused Power. "

Think of a time when someone who had been given power by others, used that power in a negative way. Maybe the person was someone you know if it was, please don't tell us his or her name. Or maybe the person was someone you read about in the newspaper or learned of in your history book. Tell us what the person did. Perhaps a boss threatened to fire his workers if they didn't do certain personal favors for him. Or may be an elected official used her position more to further her political career than to serve the people who elected her. Have you ever told someone a secret and found out later that the person bragged about having the information in order to look important in front of others? Is it a misuse of power to bribe someone with the promise of a wonderful reward in order to get him to do something dangerous or illegal? Think about it for a few moments. Then describe an incident like this and tell us how you think it affected everyone involved. The topic is, "A Time Someone Misused Power.

Discussion Questions:

1. *Why do people misuse or abuse power?*

2. *How do you feel when someone you entrust with power misuses it? What can you do?*

3. *Who suffers when a leader misuses his or her power?*

4. *What are ethics? What does it mean to act in an ethical way?*

5. *How will you use the ideas shared in this activity?*

I Time I Talked to Someone
I Was Afraid to Talk To
A Sharing Circle

Objectives:

The students will:
— describe incidents in which they overcame a fear of communicating.
— identify effective techniques for interacting with persons in authority.

Introduce the Topic:

Today we're going to talk about one of the most common and familiar fears among people, teenagers, little kids, and adults alike—one that many people think they alone experience! Our topic is, "A Time I Talked to Someone I Was Afraid to Talk To.

We have all had the experience of being around someone who caused us to feel scared, or overwhelmed, or nervous. Think of a time when this happened to you. Perhaps the person was very important, or very accomplished, or had authority over you in some way. Ordinarily, you may have avoided contact with this individual. But for some reason, which you can explain to us, one particular day you decided that you were going to talk to him/her. Maybe you absolutely had to speak to this person about something there was simply no getting out of it. Or maybe you just decided to see if you could do it. If you share, tell us what you did and how you felt about it. However, if there's anything negative involved, please don't tell us the name of the person. The topic is, "A Time I Talked to Someone I Was Afraid to Talk To.

Discussion Questions:

1. *How did this person act toward you when you talked to him or her?*

2. *What feelings did you have before and after you actually spoke to the person?*

3. *What are we afraid of when we avoid talking to people who have authority?*

4. *Many people in authority—like principals, elected officials, doctors, employers need and want to talk to people. How do you think they would react if they knew so many people were afraid to interact with them?*

5. *What skills could we learn that would make it easier for us to talk to people in authority?*

What I Think Makes a Meeting Work
A Sharing Circle

Objectives:

The students will:
— describe types and styles of meetings they prefer.
— identify ingredients of successful meetings.

Introduce the Topic:

All of us have attended meetings, and some of us have led them. Each of us has ideas about what a successful meeting looks and feels like. Today we're going to share those ideas. The topic is, "What I Think Makes a Meeting Work. "

What kinds of meetings do you like to attend? Do you enjoy a meeting that is loosely organized and relaxed, even though sometimes not much gets done? Or do you favor a no-nonsense meeting that follows "Robert's Rules of Order?" Maybe you like small meetings where a few people really get down and try to solve a problem. Or maybe you prefer attending big meetings where you can disappear into the crowd and just enjoy watching. Perhaps your favorite kind of meeting is one at which people actually do something, instead of talking all the time. Think about it for a few moments. If it helps, tell us about a specific meeting that you enjoyed. Include the name of the organization, what your role was, and what you appreciated about the meeting. The topic is, " What I Think Makes a Meeting Work

Discussion Questions:

1. *What kinds of meetings did most of us prefer?*

2. *What specific ingredients made those meetings work?*

3. *Why do people meet, anyway?*

4. *If you could change one thing about the meetings you attend now, what would it be?*

5. *As a leader, what will you do to make your own meetings work?*

SELF DETERMINATION AND PERSONAL MASTERY

To engage in self determination, young people must learn to be assertive. They must understand that it is appropriate to ask questions when clarification is necessary, and to put forth their views regarding issues and problems. They must also respect the rights of others to do the same. People who engage in self determination usually have high self esteem. That is, they understand that they make a difference and that they have something to contribute.

Closely linked to self determination is self advocacy. Young people must understand that they are capable, and that they affect and direct their own lives. No advocate will ever have the dedication, determination, or vested interest as great as the one who is advocating for him or herself. This unit focuses on building self concept and self esteem, and on developing the assertive skills necessary for self determination and self advocacy, all attributes of successful people and effective leaders.

Measuring Success
Experience Sheet and Discussion

Objectives:

The students will
— identify specific ways in which they limit themselves.
— describe how self limitations are formed and ways they can be eliminated.

Materials:

a copy of the experience sheet, "Success Takes Guts" for each student; whiteboard or chart paper

Directions:

Pass out the experience sheet, "Success Takes Guts." Give the students a couple of minutes to read the story, "The Jar of Fleas." Elicit the reactions of the students, helping them view the story as analogous to situations in which people fail because they don't expect to succeed in the first place. Point out that there are, from time to time, real lids on our lives that keep us from doing things we could otherwise do, just as there really was a lid on the jar of fleas for awhile. However, things change, and all too often we think there are lids above us that aren't there anymore.

Ask the students to think of ways in which they limit themselves. Write some of their suggestions on the board.

Give the students a few minutes to complete the experience sheet. Have them share their responses in dyads. Lead a culminating discussion.

Discussion Questions:

1. *Can you think of a mistake you've made only once? What was it? How do you feel about eliminating that mistake?*

2. *Why do we fear criticism?*

3. *How can we develop an ability to listen to criticism without feeling mortally wounded each time?*

4. *Why do some of us remember our mistakes and failures better than we remember our successes? How can we reverse that tendency?*

Success Takes Guts
Experience Sheet

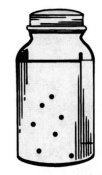

The Jar of Fleas

Old Harry Fretchit wanted to train some new fleas for his flea circus, so he hung out with some cats and dogs until he caught about ten nice, strong, high-jumping fleas. Harry wanted fleas that were strong and healthy, so the higher they jumped, the better. But you can't train a flea who can jump clear across the room without first getting its attention.

So high jumping was the first habit of Harry's new fleas that he had to break. How he did it was very interesting.

At first, the fleas were in a big cage where they had plenty of jumping room. So Harry patiently transferred them to a jar about five inches high. After that, each time a flea jumped, he banged his whole body on the lid of the jar. Obviously, continual body banging felt very uncomfortable to the fleas. As a result, they began to jump with less vigor, so that when they banged themselves it wouldn't hurt so bad (but it still hurt). After a while, they jumped with even *less* vigor, until finally one flea made a very weak jump and went down again without banging himself at all! As soon as the other fleas saw this, they copied him, and pretty soon all of the fleas were jumping up and down inside the jar without hitting the lid.

Harry had been watching, but he didn't take the lid off—yet. He wanted the fleas to get so used to having the lid there, and jumping little jumps, that they wouldn't miss the lid after it was gone. They would not even *remember* how to make big jumps.

And that's exactly what happened. After several more days, Harry took off the lid and, sure enough, there were those poor little fleas jumping up and down, but never higher than four-and-three-quarters inches for the rest of their lives.

Take a look. Are there any imaginary lids above you?

Write down some of the ways you limit yourself.

1. _____

_____

_____

2. _____

_____

_____

3. _____

_____

_____

Just in case, like the fleas, you've forgotten some of *your* capabilities, take the time to remember them now. Complete the following sentences:

I did something during the first five years of my life that was successful. It was:

_____

During the time I was in elementary school, I succeeded at:

_____

When I was in middle school, one of my successes was:

_____

Since I've been in high school, I've succeeded at:

_____

Something I can show other people how to do is:

_____

I am admired by someone for my ability to:

_____

A game I usually win is: _____

_____

The subject I'm best at in school is:

_____

I feel very proud of myself when I:

_____

_____

A job or duty I'm good at is: _____

_____

A positive habit I've got that I'm pleased with is:

_____

Five things I like about myself are:

1._____

2._____

3._____

4._____

5._____

Some people limit themselves because they fear criticism. Other people fear failure. Quite a few fear both. If you fit any of these categories, try to remember to:
1. See and believe in each one of your achievements.
2. Exercise your right to accept or reject criticism based on its worth and value to you.
3. Accept failure as an occasional price of trying.

In Search of the Perfect Person
Experiment and Discussion

Objectives:

The students will:
— state that there are no perfect people.
— identify examples of perfectionistic thinking.
— describe how perfectionism erodes self esteem and esteem for others.
— challenge perfectionistic thinking in themselves and others.

Materials:

at least four of the following: pictures of Presidents of the United States, movie stars, baseball players, or different types of dogs or cats; collections of apples, pears, marbles, rocks, or other slightly different items of the same class or type

Directions:

Place the items chosen on a table and ask a few students at a time to come up and examine them very carefully. After the students have had a chance to study the items, ask the following questions (modified to suit the items chosen):

— *Which of the Presidents do you think was the most perfect President?*
— *Which one of the apples (pears, etc.) is the most perfect apple?*
— *Which one of the marbles (rocks, etc.) is the most perfect example of a marble?*
— *Which movie start is the most perfect of all movie stars?*

Ask the students whether they know why they are attempting to find the best example from the different groups of items. Elicit from them the fact that there are many fine examples in each group, and no one example is absolutely perfect.

Point out that since being perfect is impossible (and not much fun), it doesn't make sense for people to think that they and others have to be perfect to be liked, successful, or happy. Ask the students to share some perfectionistic ideas that might keep them from feeling good about themselves and others. For example:

• If I don't get all A's, I'm no good.
• If I'm not beautiful/handsome, no one will ever go out with me.
• If I'm clumsy, everyone will laugh at me.
• If I don't win the election, I'm not popular..

Bring up the idea that students can help one another develop positive self esteem by challenging perfectionistic ideas in the group. For example:

- "Mike, just because you've lost the student council election doesn't mean you shouldn't try out for the debate team. Look how well you share your ideas and make us all start thinking."
- "Cheryl, you seemed embarrassed after telling us you have epilepsy. It's difficult to let others know about things like that, but you're still the same person you've always been."
- "Ann, just because you're heavy doesn't mean you can't sing with a band. You have a terrific voice."

Ask whether the students are willing to challenge perfectionistic thinking in themselves and in other group members when they see it.

Discussion Questions:

1. *How many perfect people have you met in your lifetime?*
2. *If you haven't met a perfect person, what do you think your chances are of meeting one in the future?*
3. *Do you think it is possible to be perfect? What would being perfect be like?*
4. *Do you think you were born with perfectionistic ideas, or did you learn them? If so, how did you learn them?*

Mastering Assertive Communication
Experience Sheet, Role Play, and Discussion

Objectives:

The students will:
- — describe the differences between assertive, aggressive, and passive behaviors.
- — practice assertive and non assertive behaviors in role play situations.

Materials:

a copy of the experience sheet, "Reacting Assertively" for each student page

Directions:

Begin by talking with the students about the fact that they have a choice whether they communicate passively, aggressively, or assertively. Point out that sometimes people act passively or aggressively because they haven't learned how to be assertive. When this is the case, it is difficult for people to get their needs met or their ideas expressed. Ask the students: "Have you ever felt taken advantage of or misunderstood? Do you think this might have happened because you weren't assertive?"

Pass out the experience sheet, "Reacting Assertively." Read the definitions of Aggressive, Passive, and Assertive together. Discuss the differences. Give some examples from your own experience. Have the students pair up, and test their ability to discriminate between the three types of responses by completing the remainder of the experience sheet. Instruct them to identify the personal rights that are being threatened or violated by the aggressive and passive responses in each example and to specify whose rights those are.

Go over the answers in the larger group. Invite some of the dyad pairs to role play the different situations. Have them role play all three responses, and then discuss the differences between the three. Facilitate discussion throughout the role plays.

Discussion Questions:

1. *How did you feel when you were being aggressive? ... passive? ... assertive?*
2. *How did you feel when you were on the receiving end of an aggressive response? ... a passive response? ... an assertive response?*
3. *How do you react when someone almost always responds aggressively, but disguises his or her responses with humor?*
4. *What causes people to respond passively?*
5. *What skills do you need to practice in order to become comfortably assertive?*

Reacting Assertively
Experience Sheet

What does it mean to be aggressive, passive, or assertive?

People are aggressive when they:
• intentionally attack, take advantage of, humiliate, hurt, or put down others.
• act on the belief that others are not as important as they are.

The aggressive person's mottos are:
"Get them before they get you."
"How you play doesn't count, only that you win."
"Never give a sucker an even break."

People are passive when they:
• invite, encourage, or permit others to take advantage of them.
• discount themselves and act as if others are more important than they are.

The passive person's mottos are:
"I should never make anyone feel uncomfortable, resentful, or displeased, except myself."
"I should never give anyone a headache or stomachache, except myself."
"I should never disappoint anyone or cause anyone to disapprove of me."

People are assertive when they:
• express themselves openly and honestly to communicate their needs, wants, or feelings, without demanding or discounting the wants, needs, or feelings of others.
• act according to the belief that all people including themselves are equally important.

The assertive person's mottos are:
"I have the right to ask for anything I want."
"If I want something and don't ask for it, I forfeit my right to complain."
"Others have an equal right to ask for what they want."
"I recognize their rights without discounting my own."

Decide which of the following responses are passive, aggressive, and assertive. What personal rights are being violated by each aggressive response? What personal rights are being violated by each passive response?

• Ms. Reynolds, John's history teacher, tells John that his homework is unacceptable, and he must redo it to get a grade. John replies:

1. "I'm so stupid. I never get anything right."
2. "No way! That's totally unfair!"
3. "I'll do the homework over, Ms. Reynolds, but I need to talk to you first, so that I'll get it right this time."

• Lydia asks her friend Alice to help her carry some things to the auditorium. Alice responds:

1. "I'm afraid I'll be late for English, but if you want me to, okay."
2. "What's the matter with you? Are your arms broken?"
3. "I can't help you right now, Lydia. I have to get to my English class."

• Tony asks Linda to go to the dance with him. Ross gets mad when he finds out, because he asked Linda, too. Ross tells Tony to back off. Tony replies:

1. "Tough! She wouldn't go with a jerk like you, anyway!"
2. "Sure, Ross. Gosh, I'm awful sorry, really."
3. "I think I have the right to ask Linda if I want to."

• Mary approaches her teacher about a low grade on a written report. She says that because of all her other activities she ran out of time. The teacher says:

1. "You only get what you earn. If you want a better grade, get your priorities straight."
2. "Oh, dear! It's my fault for not realizing how busy everyone is."
3. "Well, that's too bad."

• Chris realizes, upon leaving the supermarket, that she has been shortchanged 65 cents. She returns, but the cashier denies the mistake. Chris says:

1. "You're a liar. Give me my 65 cents right now!"
2. "Well, um, I guess I must have miscounted. Sorry to bother you."
3. "I'm sure about this. Here, count the change yourself."

• Andy returns a pair of jeans to the store because the zipper is broken. The clerk says:
1. "Yes, that's a broken zipper all right. Can I get you another pair?"
2. "Oh, I'm so sorry. I should have checked the jeans before I sold them to you. It's all my fault."
3. "You broke this zipper didn't you? Well, you're not going to cheat us!"

• Barbara drives into the parking lot of a small mall, but all the handicapped spaces are taken, so she has to park in a regular spot and then struggle to remove her chair from the back seat. As she's passing one of the handicapped spaces, Barbara almost collides with a young man running to his car. She says:
1. "Thanks to you, Mister, I just had to struggle for 20 minutes getting out of my car. Maybe when you have to pay a fine, you'll stop being so selfish."
2. "Hi. I guess maybe you didn't notice that's a handicapped spot?"
3. "You violate my rights when you take a spot that's reserved for people with disabilities. I hope you won't do it again."

• David's parents have outlined some chores for him to do around the house and yard, but he's fallen behind. His dad threatens to ground David if he doesn't meet his responsibilities before the weekend. David says:
1. "I guess I'm just a worthless slob."
2. "You're trying to make my life miserable. This is abuse. You'll be sorry!"
3. "I've been concerned about the chores, too. I'll rearrange my schedule and get them done."

• When she comes home from work, Dan's mother brings his bike in out of the rain. When Dan thanks her, she says:
1. "Oh, don't thank me. I'm gone so much of the time, I should thank you for even being here."
2. "If you weren't such a moron, you wouldn't have left it out in the rain in the first place."
3. "I'm glad I could help you."

228

Resisting Pressure
Presentation, Discussion, and Writing

Objectives:

The students will:
— describe peer pressure situations they have experienced.
— identify needs and desires to which pressuring peers appeal.
— learn personal and social skills for resisting the influence of peers and negative role models.

Materials:

a copy of the experience sheet, "Responding to Peer Pressure" for each student; whiteboard or chart paper

Directions:

In large letters on the board, write the heading, "Peer Pressure." Remind the students of the many people and things that influence their decisions. Point out that peer pressure is one type of influence that can cause decisions to be hard to make. Ask, "What very strong need does peer pressure usually appeal to?" When the students describe the following need, write it on the board:

Peer pressure appeals to a person's desire to fit in and be accepted by a group.

Discuss the differences between positive and negative peer pressure. Explain that peer pressure can influence people to make healthy, productive choices, and it can influence them to do things that are illegal, unhealthy, dangerous, or simply at odds with their beliefs, preferences, or values.

Ask the students to brainstorm different styles of peer pressure. For example: *Friendly, teasing, intimidating, guilt producing, humiliating, verbally abusive, demanding, bribing, threatening, and physically menacing.*

Discuss each type of pressure. Invite the students to think of verbal statements that illustrate each type. For example:

Friendly: *Come on, be a pal and..*
Teasing: *It's okay, we all know you can't handle your liquor..*
Intimidating: *If you know what's good for you, you'll...*
Guilt producing: *If you were really my friend, you'd..*
Humiliating: *You don't know anything you're a retard!*
Bribing: *I'll take out the trash for a week if you'll...*
Threatening: *If you don't do it, I'll tell Mom...*

Ask the students what questions they can ask themselves when deciding whether or not to go along with peer pressure. Write their ideas on the board or chart paper. Add these questions if the students don't generate them:

— What are they asking me to do?
— Do I really want to do it?
— What are the consequences of doing it?
— Does doing this fit with my beliefs, values, and/or goals?
— Is doing this really good for me?
— If not, what other choices do I have?

Pass out the experience sheet, "Responding to Peer Pressure." Ask the students to close their eyes and think of a peer pressure situation that is happening in their life now, or has happened recently. After a few moments, ask them to open their eyes and write a brief description of the situation on the experience sheet. Give the students 5 to 10 minutes to answer the remaining questions on the sheet.

Offer the students an opportunity to discuss what they have written with a partner. Respect the wishes of those who prefer to keep their written statements private. Facilitate a follow-up discussion.

Discussion Questions:

1. *What kinds of pressure are the most difficult to deal with? Why?*

2. *What seems to work in these situations?*

3. *Why don't people take no for an answer?*

4. *Why is it so hard at times to resist a friend?*

5. *If a friend gets mad at you for resisting his/her pressure, what can you do about it?*

Responding to Peer Pressure
Experience Sheet

It's normal to want to fit in and feel accepted and liked. Sometimes this need is so strong, we are tempted to do almost anything to satisfy it — including things we shouldn't do. When other kids try to get you to do something that is wrong or dangerous, it's called *peer pressure*.

Think of a peer-pressure situation that is happening in your life right now. Or think of one that has happened in the past. Write a brief description of the situation here:

_____

_____

_____

_____

Now answer these questions:

1. What are your peers asking you to do?

_____

_____

_____

_____

2. Do you really want to do it?

_____

_____

_____

3. What are the consequences of doing it? What might happen to you and other people if you do it?

_____

_____

_____

4. Does doing this fit with your beliefs, values, and/or goals? How?

_____

_____

_____

5. Is doing this really good for you? How will you benefit?

_____

_____

_____

6. If not, what other choices do you have?

_____

_____

Something I Enjoy Doing Because It Gives Me a Feeling of Accomplishment
A Sharing Circle

Objectives:

The students will:
— identify strengths, talents, and special abilities in self and others.
— practice methods of positive self talk.
— describe how positive self talk enhances self esteem.

Introduce the Topic:

One of the most powerful motivators for doing something is anticipating the feeling of accomplishment that we experience when the task is finished. Today, we're going to take a mental inventory of our activities and identify one that we can always depend on to give us a sense of pride and achievement. Our topic is, "Something I Enjoy Doing Because It Gives Me a Feeling of Accomplishment. "

Think of something you enjoy doing at school or elsewhere that really causes you to feel as though you've accomplished something. It can be a task you've completed only once, or something you do regularly. Perhaps you get enjoyment out of working with computers and feel good each time you successfully develop a step in some new program or application. Maybe you enjoy drawing because every completed picture is a proud new creation. Or maybe you enjoy holding office, because every time you successfully conduct a meeting or organize an activity, you know others benefit from your efforts. Does cooking give you feelings of accomplishment? Do you like to solve math problems or complete science experiments? Think about it for a minute. The topic is, "Something I Enjoy Doing Because It Gives Me a Feeling of Accomplishment.

Discussion Questions:

1. *Why is it important to accomplish things?*

2. *What do accomplishments have to do with self esteem?*

3. *What are some examples of small, everyday accomplishments?*

4. *How can you use self talk to remind yourself of your accomplishments?*

My Greatest Strength
A Sharing Circle

Objectives:

The students will:
— recognize and describe their own worth and worthiness.
— identify strengths, talents, and special abilities in self and others.
— practice methods of positive self talk.

Introduce the Topic:

We all have both strengths and weaknesses, but unfortunately, too often we focus on the weaknesses. Today, we're going to think and talk about our strengths. Our topic is, "My Greatest Strength.

Tell us about a talent or ability that you're particularly proud of. Maybe it's your sense of humor, or how you can solve problems, or your ability in music. Or maybe it has to do with the way you relate to other people. For example, perhaps you are a very good listener, or especially friendly, or adept at organizing and leading groups of people. In this session, you have permission to boast. Think this over for a minute. The topic is, "My Greatest Strength. "

Discussion Questions:

1. *How do you feel when you talk about your strengths?*

2. *Where do we get the notion that it's undesirable to talk about our positive qualities?*

3. *What are the benefits in stating your strengths?*

4. *If you are trying to strengthen an ability or learn a new skill, how can you use self talk to your advantage?*

It Was Hard to Say No, But I Did
A Sharing Circle

Objectives:

The students will:
— describe the use of refusal skills.
— demonstrate an understanding of assertive, aggressive, and passive behaviors and their consequences in dealing with peer pressure.

Introduce the Topic:

Today, we're going to talk about times when we were assertive, when we made our own decision and stood up for our wants and needs. Today's topic is, "It Was Hard to Say No, But I Did."

Can you think of a time when you said no, even though it was difficult? Maybe a friend tried to talk you into going to a movie instead of finishing your homework and, though tempted, you said no. Maybe some kids offered you a drug and tried to make you feel like a wimp when you refused, but you decided your health was more important than your image and held your ground. Or maybe some friends were planning a prank for their own amusement but at someone else's expense, and you stayed out of it. Have you ever been tempted to cut school, but said no? Have you ever refused someone who offered to trade answers on an exam? Have you ever been the only one to vote "no" on an issue that you thought was being handled poorly? Think it over for a minute and then tell us about a time like this in your life. The topic is, "It Was Hard to Say No, But I Did."

Discussion Questions:

1. *What were your feelings just before you said no?*

2. *How do you feel about it now?*

3. *What methods of saying no work best for you?*

4. *What do you gain personally by standing up for your beliefs or your rights?*

5. *Why is peer pressure so difficult to resist?*

EXPLORING CAREERS

It is vitally important that students be encouraged to view themselves from as many different perspectives as possible before they begin to look at career options. As they gain insight into their capabilities and limitations; interests and disinterests; and skills and preferences, they can more clearly and objectively see career choices as exciting and challenging, rather than as overwhelming mysteries that seem unattainable or out of reach.

The activities in this unit will allow students to assess personal aptitudes, interests, and abilities. With this information they will choose alternatives and make decisions to plan and pursue tentative educational and career goals. They will also relate careers to the needs and functions of the economy and society and apply skills to locate, understand, and use career information.

Discover Your Skills
Experience Sheet and Discussion

Objectives:

The student will:
— assess personal aptitudes, interests, and abilities relative to career possibilities.
— relate educational achievement to career opportunities.

Materials:

pens or pencils, and one copy of the experience sheet, "Activities, Skills, and Likes" for each student; whiteboard

Directions:

Begin by writing the headings, Activities, Skills, and Likes above three separate columns on the board.

Point out that people engage in numerous activities every day. Inherent in each activity are skills that must be employed in order to accomplish the activity. For example: Skiing is an activity that requires the skills of **balance**, **coordination**, and **spatial perception**. What we like about skiing may be the **scenic beauty** of the mountain, the **company**, **exercise**, **competition**, etc. Using the columns on the board, develop two or three other examples, listing the skills and probable likes inherent in each.

Distribute the experience sheets. Explain that you want the students to each develop a personal activity list, following the example on the board. Suggest that they try to fill the column with activities. As they work, individually assist the students to identify the skills involved in their respective activities and to write these in the second column. Then walk the class through the coding process. Explain: *In the third column, write "O" if the activity takes place <u>outdoors</u>, "I" if the activity takes place <u>indoors</u>, or "O/I" if the activity takes place either outdoors or indoors. In the fourth column, write "A" if you do the activity <u>alone</u>, "O" if you do it with <u>others</u>, or "A/O" if you can do it either alone or with others. In the last column, write "L" if you <u>like</u> the activity and "D" if you <u>dislike</u> the activity.*

Next, on the second page have students list their required and elective school subjects. Again, assist them with the coding process, by explaining: *Look over the list carefully and choose your <u>best</u> subject. Place a plus mark beside it. Next, decide which is your <u>worst</u> subject and indicate it with a minus. Finally, choose your <u>favorite</u> subject and place a star beside it. If your favorite subject is also the one at which you do best, that subject will have two marks beside it. Think carefully when making your choices. Don't confuse your feelings for a course with your feelings for the teacher of the course—they are not the same.*

Finally, ask the students to complete the statements at the bottom of the page for their best, worst, and favorite subjects. For example:

- *My best subject is Math because I learn math concepts easily and get A's on all my tests.*
- *My worst subject is Art because I don't draw well and, compared to talented kids in the class, my work always pulls a C.*
- *My favorite subject is Physical Education because I'm on the track team and I love to run.*

Allow time for volunteers to share discoveries from their lists, and then lead a group discussion.

Discussion Questions:

1. *What kinds of activities did you list?*
2. *What skills are inherent in your activities?*
3. *What skills did you list that you haven't developed yet? Are you working on them? How?*
4. *What kinds of jobs might utilize these skills?*
5. *How many of you seem to prefer outdoor activities? ...indoor activities?*
6. *How many of you seem to prefer independent activities? ...group activities?*
7. *How might these factors affect your choice of a career?*
8. *Why is it important to consider the kinds of activities you like when you are thinking about what kind of career you want to prepare for?*

Activities, Skills, and Likes
Experience Sheet

Activities	Skills	Outdoors or Indoors	Alone or with Other	Like or Dislike

**List Your Required
and Elective School
Subjects**

	Best	Worst	Favorite

My best subject is _____ **because**

_____

_____

My worst subject is _____ **because**

_____

_____

My favorite subject is _____ **because**

_____

_____

When Money Counts
Research and Discussion

Objectives:

The student will:
— apply skills in locating, understanding, and using career information.
— identify types and levels of work performed across a broad range of occupations.
— relate careers to the needs and functions of the economy and society.

Materials:

paper, pens or pencils, and the Occupational Outlook Handbook, (available both in print or online; whiteboard

Directions:

Begin by asking the students what careers or jobs they think they might like to have in the future. Elicit several responses. When students mention categories instead of specific jobs, jot the categories down on the board. For example, *law* is a category within which there are many different jobs, only one of which is *lawyer* (and there are many different types of lawyers). Likewise, teacher, artist, and business manager might be considered categories. Teaching skills, for example, are used by school teachers at all levels, college professors, corporate and military trainers, health professionals, fitness trainers, recreational specialists, salespeople, etc. Urge the students to be open to examining the enormous variety of specific jobs within any one category.

Next, working individually, have the students make a list of careers or jobs they might like to have.

Introduce the students to the *Occupational Outlook Handbook.*

Explain that the handbook lists thousands of job titles, along with the salary range, education/training requirements, and current/projected outlook (demand) for each job. Show the students how the handbook is organized. Help them to use the handbook to locate the careers/jobs on their individual lists, writing down the salary, education/ training, and outlook for each job. In addition, suggest that for every job on their list, they find two related jobs of which they were previously unaware, and add these to their list, too.

When the students have completed their examination of the handbook and finished their information search, conduct a discussion about their findings.

Discussion Questions:

1. *What new jobs did you identify?*
2. *Which jobs require the most education/training?*
3. *What relationship did you discover between education/training and salaries?*
4. *What kinds of jobs seem to have the best outlook? ...the worst outlook?*
5. *What was the most unusual job title you saw?*
6. *What need or function does the job of _____ fill in society?*

Picture This . . .
Brainstorming and Discussion

Objectives:

The student will:
— make decisions and choose alternatives in planning and pursuing career goals.
— understand the interrelationship of life goals and careers.

Materials:

one copy of the experience sheet, "Picture This" for each student; information generated from the activity, "When Money Counts"

Directions:

Begin by explaining that when we have a picture of the kind of lifestyle we desire, we can better develop and direct our career plans.

Pass out the "Picture This" worksheet. Go over the directions. Elicit some examples of values, goals, family goals, and skills. List them on the board. Give the students time to complete the first page of the experience sheets. Circulate and offer assistance to individual students, as needed.

Ask the students to turn to the second page. Note that while the first page asked for characteristics about the students, page two lists characteristics of jobs. Tell the students to circle one or two items in each category to get a picture of conditions under which they prefer to work.

Have the students pair up and take turns sharing the information generated with a partner.

Finally, have the students compare the job information gathered through the activity, "When Money Counts" with the choices made in this activity. Tell them to identify the two jobs/careers that appear to best satisfy these combined criteria. When the students have made their decisions, lead a class discussion.

Discussion Questions:

1. *What connections did you discover between your personal goals and your job goals? ...your family goals and your job goals? ...your skills and your job goals?*

2. *What career choices look promising?*

3. *What are some important issues to consider when making career choices?*

4. *Which of your choices appeared to be in conflict?*

Picture This . . .
Experience Sheet

Directions: In each category, list things that are true *for you*. List things you **value**, like travel, exercise, beautiful surroundings, friends, etc. List future **goals**, like graduating from college, owning a home, buying a particular car, etc. List **family goals**, such as when (and if) you want to marry, have children, etc. Finally, list some of your **skills**, **aptitudes**, and **interests**.

Values	Goals

Family Goals	Skills, Aptitudes, Interests

Now Picture This . . .

Directions: In each category, circle two or three items that describe the job conditions *you* prefer.

Rewards	**Level of Responsibility**
High Pay	No Decisions
Excitement	Some Decisions
Commissions	Decision Maker
Responsibility	Own Boss
Recognition	Work for Someone
Adventure	Team Effort
Security	Creativity
Risk	Limited Stress
Flexible Time	Power
Emotional Satisfaction	Freedom
Other _____	Other _____
Place	**Working with**
Indoor	No one else
Outdoor	Many others
Office	Adults
Home	Children
Shop	Senior Citizens
Warehouse	Animals
Garage	Information
Hospital	Things
School	Hands
Church	Art
Factory	Machines
Other _____	Other _____

What Do I Want to Be When I Grow Up?
Research

Objectives:

The student will:
— relate educational achievement to career opportunities.
— research, evaluate and interpret information about career opportunities.
— apply skills to locate, understand, and use career information.

Materials:

Dictionary of Occupational Titles (available online), various career materials from the library, previous completed experience sheets, and two copies of the worksheet, "Gathering Career Information" for each student

Directions:

Review the steps taken and information gathered in the previous career activities. Announce that in this activity, each student will gather in-depth information about the two career choices made in the activity, "Picture This."

Distribute two copies of the experience sheets so the students can complete an experience sheet on each of the two career choices they made in the previous activity. Note that some of the information called for on the sheets has already been obtained in previous exercises. Show, and/or list on the board sources for obtaining additional information. Circulate and assist the students while they complete the experience sheets. When the students have finished, lead a class discussion.

Discussion Questions:

1. *How likely are you to pursue one of the careers you researched?*

2. *What information surprised or concerned you?*

3. *What will be the most difficult part of obtaining your career goal?*

4. *Are you more or less interested in this career now that you have a greater familiarity with it?*

Gathering Career Information
Experience Sheet

Choose a job title for one career choice. Fill in "Job Title." Then, answer the questions about the job as completely and specifically as you can with the available resources.

Job Title _____

1. List specific duties performed in the job.

_____

_____

_____

2. Where is the job performed? (Indoors, outdoors, office, factory, etc.)

_____

_____

3. What makes the job particularly appealing to you?

_____

_____

_____

4. What kinds of rewards does the job offer?

_____

_____

5. How much education or training is required for this job?

_____

_____

_____

6. Where could you receive the necessary training or education?

_____

_____

_____

7. What are the physical requirements, if any?

_____

_____

_____

8. What is the approximate starting salary? ...the approximate mid-career salary?

_____

_____

9. Will the number of jobs available in this field by the time you are prepared to enter the job market be low, moderate, or high?

_____

_____

_____

10. What special talents or abilities are required for the job?

_____

_____

_____

11. What can you do <u>now</u> to begin preparing for the job?

_____

_____

_____

12. What high school classes will help you prepare for the job?

_____

_____

_____

13. In what geographical areas of the state/nation/world is the job available?

_____

_____

_____

Expertly Speaking
Interviews and Discussion

Objectives:

The student will:
— research, evaluate and interpret information about career opportunities.
— choose alternatives and make decisions to plan and pursue tentative educational and career goals.

Materials:

two Expertly Speaking interview worksheets for each student

Directions:

Introduce the activity by saying to the students: *One valuable way to gain insight into a career is to interview someone who is already doing the job you're interested in. Such a person can offer information not easily found in resource materials. Many employment counselors and career experts recommend this approach. Since most people like to talk about themselves as well as help others, they are often willing to give informational interviews to students.*

Students who already know someone working in their field of interest can contact that person. If they do not know someone, suggest that they consult a teacher, fellow students, parents, professional organizations, unions, employment offices, the librarian, the Chamber of Commerce, service clubs such as Rotary, Lions, etc., or the yellow pages of the telephone directory.

Elicit from the students suggestions concerning how to contact prospective interviewees. Here are some examples:

- State your name and school clearly.
- Describe the purpose of your call.
- Describe the reason for the interview.
- Schedule a specific time for the interview.
- Obtain directions, if necessary.

Remind the students that business and professional people usually maintain busy schedules and that, on the day of the interview, they should:

- Plan to be prompt.
- Dress appropriately.
- Terminate the interview at the agreed upon time.
- Introduce themselves, shake hands, be polite, maintain eye contact throughout the interview, and do more listening than talking.

Following the interviews, allow class time for sharing and discussion.

Discussion Questions:

1. *Which aspects of the job were in keeping with the information you gathered through your research? ...which differed?*

2. *What was the most interesting piece of information you learned from the interview?*

3. *How has your attitude about this job changed?*

Note: Designate class time for writing thank-you notes to the interviewees.

Expertly Speaking
Interview Worksheet

Name: _____

Job Title: _____

How many years have you worked in this profession? _____

Describe your educational background and preparation. _____

_____

_____

Would you do anything differently if you had an opportunity to live your educational years over again? If so, what? _____

_____

_____

What do you feel would be the best approach for me to prepare for this career?

_____

_____

_____

How does this career fit into the needs and functions of the economy and society? _____

_____

_____

What is the best and the worst aspect for you about this job? _____

_____

_____

Did you work in any other job/career prior to this one? If so, what, and did it lead to this one? _____

_____

_____

Do you feel you will experience a career change before you retire? If so, what would the change be? _____

Getting From Here to There
Research and Sharing Groups

Objective:

The students will research, evaluate and interpret information concerning the expenses of post high-school education, and the financial resources available to meet those expenses.

Materials:

a variety of college catalogs (both 2- and 4-year); brochures and catalogs from technical schools, business schools, and branches of the military; samples of bulletins and financial-aid information from all types of colleges and vocational/technical schools; and one copy of the experience sheet, "Getting From Here to There," for each student

Directions:

Distribute the experience sheets. Go over them with the students. In your own words, say: *Based on your research, you have a pretty clear picture of the education and/ or training needed for the career you desire. Whatever career choice you make will probably require money, and that can be discouraging if your resources are limited. Examine the catalogs and brochures to gain a clearer picture of the costs of education and/or training. Then, using the experience sheet for your notes, figure the expense of tuition and fees, books and supplies, room and board, transportation, and personal expenses such as clothing, laundry, entertainment, etc. Add up all expenses to reach an approximate total figure. Then estimate your income from all sources. Subtract your income estimate from your expense estimate. The balance is the amount that you must finance through scholarships, loans, or employment.*

Encourage the students to read about different sources of financial aid. Explore with them various options available for financing an education. Here are some examples:

- **Scholarships** and **grants** that do not have to be repaid. Some are based on financial need, others on scholastic achievement, athletics, or special ability in the arts.

- **Loans**, which must be paid back, usually with interest. Educational loans frequently have lower interest rates; repayment begins after graduation.
- The **military** offers opportunities for education and training, both during and after a period of enlistment.
- Full or part-time **employment**. Completing an education this way takes longer, but does not entail the repayment of loans.

Extension:

Have each student request information and application materials from at least three sources of financial aid. Help them choose sources that are appropriate to their tentative college/technical school choices. On a specific date, have the students bring their materials to class and share them. Group the students according to whether their information primarily addresses the military, 4-year colleges, community colleges, or technical/trade schools. Following a discussion period, have each group report its findings to the class.

Getting From Here to There
Experience Sheet

Looking through catalogs and brochures, examine two colleges or trade schools you could attend to obtain your career goal. Using the figures you find, fill in the two columns for each with the approximate amounts for the items listed to determine the cost of one year's schooling/training. Then, estimate your sources of income and fill in the blanks.

Estimate of Yearly Expenses	College/ Trade School	College/ Trade School
Tuition & fees	$	$
Books & supplies		
Room & Board		
Transportation		
Personal		
Entertainment		
Miscellaneous		
TOTAL	$	$
Sources of Yearly Income		
Savings	$	$
Parent contribution		
Summer work		
Other		
TOTAL	$	$

Subtract total income from total expenses to determine the amount of financial aid needed.

How Most People Get Jobs!
A Networking Activity

Objectives:

The students will:
— explain and demonstrate the use of networking to reach employment goals.
— define networking and state why it works.

Materials:

one copy of the experience sheet, "Does Networking Really Work?" for each student; the following chart drawn on a large piece of chart paper or on the board:

Maria	Tom	Mr. Harris	Mrs. Gomez
Wants a part-time job. Enjoys small children.	Needs transportation 5 miles a day to his job in Putville.	Owns a pizza shop. Needs a delivery person.	Wants to sell a dining room set.
Dave	Susanna	Bob	Dennis
Sandy	Terri	Jack	Jan
Joe	Sal & Nancy	Angie	Lee
Makes two deliveries each day to Putville, morning and afternoon.	Got married last month. They need a dining room set.	Has two small children. Needs a baby-sitter.	Has a car and needs a part-time job.

Directions:

Ask the students if they have ever heard the word "networking," and talk with them about its meaning and importance. Explain that when researchers asked thousands of people how they got their jobs, sixty to eighty percent answered by saying they received help (a tip, good advice, recommendations, etc.) from friends, family members, former co-workers, etc. The word *networking* may be a bit overused, but it's a handy one. It means *soliciting the assistance of other people to reach a personal goal.* Explain that the activity the students are about to do illustrates how networking is done. Later, the students will conduct their own research to establish how well networking works in the real world.

Introduce the chart and explain: *Here's how a network works. The people in Rows 1 and 4 have wants and needs. But they don't even know each other. The people in Row 1 only know the people in Row 2. The people in Row 2 only know the people in Rows 1 and 3. The people in Row 3 only know the people in Rows 2 and 4. The people in Row 4 only know the people in Row 3. So, in order for the people in Rows 1 and 4 to find each other, they have to get help from the people in Rows 2 and 3.*

Using the chart as a visual aid, and drawing lines from Maria to Dennis to Terri to Angie, read the students the following story about Maria, the first person in Row One:

Maria is a senior in high school and is looking for a way to earn some extra money. She really likes small children and would enjoy babysitting, but she just moved to the area and doesn't know very many people. One day, Maria meets Dennis in the hall. He lives in one of the other apartments on her floor. He says, "Hi," and they begin to talk.

Dennis is married and in his twenties. Maria asks him, "Do you and your wife have any children?"

"No, we don't," he responds. But Maria doesn't give up. She asks him if he knows anyone with children who might need a baby-sitter.

Dennis thinks for a minute and says, "Yeah. I have a sister, Terri, who lives two blocks away. She doesn't have kids either, but a lot of people in her building do and she knows them. I'll tell her to call you, okay?"

Maria thinks for a moment. She likes what she is hearing but she wants to keep control of this situation herself. She smiles and says, "Thanks. Would it be okay with you if I called her myself?"

"No problem," says Dennis.

Maria asks Dennis to wait for a moment. She darts back into her apartment and quickly returns with pencil and paper. She writes down Terri's number and thanks Dennis warmly.

"Good luck," says Dennis. "Let me know what happens."

"I sure will," Maria answers. Then she goes inside and calls the number. She hears a young woman's voice and asks, "Is this Terri?"

The woman says, "Yes, it is. Who is this?"

Then Maria says, "Terri, my name is Maria Martinez and I live in the building your brother Dennis lives in. Dennis and I were just talking and he gave me your name and number. I'm new to the area and I'm looking for some babysitting work. Dennis said you don't have any children but you live in a building with some families that do. Do you have any friends in the building I might call to see if they could use a baby-sitter?"

"What a coincidence!" says Terri. "I sure do. My friend, Angie, in the next apartment just asked me yesterday if I knew anyone who might be able to baby-sit for her three nights a week when she goes to class. I'll tell her to call you. What's your phone number?"

Maria realizes that it's a good idea to give Terri her phone number, but she knows that Terri might not see Angie for a few days, or she might even forget. "My number is 452-8977." she says. Then she adds, "This is great! Do you, by any chance, have Angie's number? I'd really like to call her myself."

Well, it all works out fine. Maria calls Angie and starts babysitting for her two days later. For the next year she baby-sits for Angie and lots of Angie's friends. And it all started the day she had that little talk with Dennis out in the hall.

Discuss the story with the students. Ask them:

1. *What did Maria do well?*
2. *What mistakes could Maria have made that she didn't make?*
3. *Would you say Maria used polite persistence? Why?*

Pick four volunteers and have them act out the story in front of the class.

Then pick three more teams of volunteer actors, with four people on each team. Have them create extemporaneous dramatic presentations of the other three situations shown on the chart.

Hold a final discussion. Ask the students the following questions:

1. *What are the key ideas this activity teaches us?*
2. *Have you ever networked before, maybe without even realizing at the time that you were networking? If so, how did it work?*

Distribute the experience sheet, "Does Networking Really Work?" and read it over with the students. Work out a realistic time frame for canvasing job holders. Set a date for tallying the results as a class.

After the class has tallied its findings and calculated the percentages, point out to the students: *These results show how many people got jobs with the help of other people. Some of them did it skillfully; others probably were not so skillful.—yet networking worked. Imagine how much higher the networking percentage would be if everyone knew how to network skillfully. That's what we've been learning how to do!*

Does Networking Really Work?
Experience Sheet

Experts who have conducted surveys report that 60% to 80% of the people in the workforce have obtained their jobs through networking. These people received help from other people. This is a very impressive percentage and some people have trouble believing it.

Why not join the other students in your class and conduct a survey? Canvas some people you know. Each time you get a response, check the line below that best matches what the person tells you.

Approach as many people with jobs as you can and ask them, "How did you get the job you have now? Did you...

See an ad in the paper or online and answer it? _____

Go to an employment agency?_____

Write a letter to the company and send along your resume?_____

Get a tip, suggestion, or a recommendation from a friend, relative, neighbor, or some other person? _____
_____

Get your job some other way? How?"

_____
_____
_____
_____
_____
_____

Tally your results.

Write your totals on the lines below. When your teacher tallies the results in class, write in the class totals in the parentheses.

How many people did you canvas?_____ (____)

How many got their jobs through each of these categories:

    Ads_____ (____)   Agencies_____ (____)

    Letters_____ (____)   Networking_____ (____)

    Other_____ (____)

Now do some math.

Figure out the percentages in each category based on the results for the entire class.

The highest percentage went to:_____ with _____ percent.

The second highest percentage went to:_____ with _____ percent.

The third highest percentage went to:_____ with _____ percent.

The lowest percentage went to:_____ with _____ percent.

Use this space for your notes:

A Skill or Talent of Mine that I Could Use in a Job
A Circle Session

Objectives:

The students will:
— assess personal aptitudes, interests, and abilities relative to career possibilities.
— apply skills to plan or revise a career plan.

Introduce the topic:

Our topic for this session is, "A Skill or Talent of Mine that I Could Use in a Job." We all have skills and talents that we use every day. Some of these skills and talents are important not only to students, but to employees in many different jobs. Perhaps you work well with people. Or maybe your strongest talent lies in dealing with information. Maybe you make friends easily, or handle confrontations tactfully and diplomatically. Perhaps you are good at solving math problems, or organizing materials. Do you like to build or repair things? Do you draw, sing, play a musical instrument, or dance well? All of these skills and talents are useful in certain jobs. Some are useful in many jobs. Tell us about a talent or skill you have and how you could use it in a job. Think it over for a few moments. The topic is, "A Skill or Talent of Mine that I Could Use in a Job."

Discussion Questions:

1. *Which skills and talents were mentioned most often?*

2. *Which skills and talents are needed in almost every kind of job?*

3. *How can knowledge of your skills and talents assist you in planning a career direction?*

A Job I Would Really Enjoy
A Circle Session

Objectives:

The students will:
— describe a job they would enjoy doing.
— demonstrate positive attitudes toward work and learning.
— relate educational achievement to career opportunities.
— relate careers to the needs and functions of the economy and society.

Introduce the topic:

Our topic for this session is, "A Job I Would Really Enjoy." There are probably many jobs you would enjoy doing. Think of one, and tell us why it appeals to you. Maybe you know you would like to be a park ranger because you love the outdoors and are interested in conservation. Perhaps you're certain you would enjoy being a robotics engineer because you have already successfully built three robots. Maybe you are fascinated with the structure of cities, so you think you would enjoy being a city planner, an architect, or an urban geographer. Maybe independence or travel are your top priorities, so you think you would enjoy being a travel writer. Perhaps you want to contribute to society by developing new sources of energy, so you hope to become a physicist. Think about it for a few moments and then tell us what job you would enjoy and why. The topic is, "One Job I Would Really Enjoy."

Discussion Questions:

1. *What similarities and differences were there among the things we shared?*

2. *Which of the jobs mentioned would require education beyond high school?*

3. *How did some of the jobs mentioned meet an important need of society?*

4. *What skills would be needed in all of the jobs that were mentioned?*

A Job I Think I Would Dislike
A Circle Session

Objective:

The students will:
— identify a job or career they don't want to pursue
— describe why it is wrong for them.

Introduce the topic:

Our topic for this session is, "A Job I Think I Would Dislike." We all want to be happy in our jobs. Consequently, we develop opinions about jobs that we think would <u>not</u> make us happy, jobs we would dislike. Can you think of a job you're almost positive you wouldn't want to have? Maybe you wouldn't want to be an accountant because to you the job sounds boring and repetitive, and you would have to work at a desk all day. Perhaps you wouldn't want to be a management consultant because you would have to travel a great deal, and continually work with strangers. Maybe the job of construction worker is not for you because it can be dirty and physically challenging. Maybe you would turn down the opportunity to become a nurse because nursing is a relatively low-paying profession. Take a few moments to think about it. The topic is, "A Job I Think I Would Dislike."

Discussion Questions:

1. *What is the major difference between the job you dislike and one you like?*

2. *How were our dislikes similar? How were they different?*

3. *How essential to the economy is the job you dislike? How essential is it to society?*

4. *What would it take to make you like the job you described?*

If I Could Do Anything, with No Limits
A Circle Session

Objectives:

The students will:
— describe what career they would choose if their possibilities were unlimited.
— describe the relationship of career to lifestyle and vise-versa.

Introduce the topic:

Our topic for this session is, "If I Could Do Anything, with No Limits." Too often, we place limits on ourselves. Sometimes those limits are realistic, but often they are not. We block ourselves because of perceived rather than real limitations. One way to discover what we really want in our lives, both personally and professionally, is to consider what we would do if we had no limitations at all. What would you want your job to be if you didn't have to worry about money, education, or training? Maybe you would be a ski instructor and live in the mountains so that your family could grow up in a natural environment. Perhaps you would like to raise horses or take care of sick animals, if you didn't have to worry about buying a ranch or paying for veterinary school. If you didn't have to worry about supporting yourself, maybe you would write a novel, or become an inventor, or work full time raising funds for the homeless. Tell us about the lifestyle and profession you would want if <u>anything</u> were possible. Take a few moments to think it over. The topic is, "If I Could Do Anything, with No Limits."

Discussion Questions:

1. *How much does a person's job determine his/her lifestyle?*

2. *Does lifestyle determine career, or does career determine lifestyle? How?*

3. *What happens when we place arbitrary limits on ourselves?*

4. *How can you plan a career that is compatible with your desired lifestyle?*

If your heart is in Social-Emotional
Learning, visit us online.

Come see us at:
www.InnerchoicePublsihing.com

Our website gives you a look at all our other Social-
Emotional Learning-based books, free activities and
learning and teaching strategies.

INNERCHOICE Publishing
15079 Oak Chase Court
Wellington, FL 33414

CPSIA information can be obtained at www.ICGtesting.com
Printed in the USA
LVOW09s2334150716

496558LV00011B/271/P